INSIDE REALITY TV

In the summer of 2010, Ragan Fox was one of twelve people selected to participate in the twelfth season of CBS's reality program *Big Brother*. Offering a rare, autobiographical, and behind-the-scenes peek behind *Big Brother*'s theatrical curtain, Fox provides a scholarly account of the show's casting procedures, secret soundstage interactions, and viewer involvement, while investigating how the program's producers, fans, and players theatrically render identities of racial and sexual minorities. Using autoethnography, textual analysis, and spectator commentary as research, *Inside Reality TV* reflects on and critiques how identity is constructed on reality television, and the various ways in which people from historically oppressed groups are depicted in mass media.

Ragan Fox is Professor of Communication at California State University, Long Beach. He is the author of two poetry collections, *Heterophobia* (2006) and *Exile in Gayville* (2009). In the summer of 2010, Fox was a contestant on the twelfth season of CBS's *Big Brother*. He currently lives in West Hollywood with his French bulldog, Beau.

INSIDE REALITY TV

Producing Race, Gender, and Sexuality on *Big Brother*

Ragan Fox

NEW YORK AND LONDON

First published 2019
by Routledge
711 Third Avenue, New York, NY 10017

and by Routledge
2 Park Square, Milton Park, Abingdon, Oxon OX14 4RN

Routledge is an imprint of the Taylor & Francis Group, an informa business

© 2019 Taylor & Francis

The right of Ragan Fox to be identified as the author of this work has been asserted by him in accordance with sections 77 and 78 of the Copyright, Designs and Patents Act 1988.

All rights reserved. No part of this book may be reprinted or reproduced or utilised in any form or by any electronic, mechanical, or other means, now known or hereafter invented, including photocopying and recording, or in any information storage or retrieval system, without permission in writing from the publishers.

Trademark notice: Product or corporate names may be trademarks or registered trademarks, and are used only for identification and explanation without intent to infringe.

Library of Congress Cataloging-in-Publication Data
Names: Fox, Ragan, author.
Title: Inside reality TV : producing race, gender, and sexuality on
   "*Big brother*" / Ragan Fox.
Description: New York : Routledge, 2018.
Identifiers: LCCN 2018018521 | ISBN 9781138065567 (hardback) |
   ISBN 9781138065574 (pbk.)
Subjects: LCSH: *Big brother* (Television program : United States) |
   Sex role on television. | Gays on television. | Fox, Ragan. |
   Television personalities—United States—Biography.
Classification: LCC PN1992.77.B495 F79 2018 |
   DDC 791.45/72—dc23
LC record available at https://lccn.loc.gov/2018018521

ISBN: 978-1-138-06556-7 (hbk)
ISBN: 978-1-138-06557-4 (pbk)
ISBN: 978-1-315-15963-8 (ebk)

Typeset in Bembo
by Apex CoVantage, LLC

Printed and bound in Great Britain by
TJ International Ltd, Padstow, Cornwall

I dedicate this book to my mother, Laura Henson, and sister, Tina Fox, both of whom spent countless hours watching me on Big Brother's *Internet feed. I am also indebted to Dr. Sharon Downey and Dr. Jessica Abrams. Their professional support and friendship enabled me to participate in* Big Brother's *twelfth season.*

CONTENTS

1	Investigating the Reality TV Paradox	1
2	"Just Be Yourself," and Other Casting Fairy Tales	24
3	"Fagan: Awesome Representative of the Gay Community"	52
Interlude		**91**
4	Performatively Spectating Houseguests of Color	95
5	Life After *Big Brother*	125
	Index	*139*

1

INVESTIGATING THE REALITY TV PARADOX

In the summer of 2010, I competed in the twelfth season of CBS's reality show *Big Brother*. New friends and professional colleagues sometimes ask what motivated me to be on a reality show. "A college professor isn't the type of person I picture on those programs," they sometimes say. I admittedly sacrificed my scholarly ethos when I hopped onto a ten-foot-tall, slippery hot dog to win power in the house. Telling a fellow houseguest that she resembled a "red-feathered parrot from hell" certainly did not help my case for tenure.

The full and suffocating weight of the "Why participate?" question felt its heaviest the morning after Season 12's finale. My department chair Amy called with an ominous message the night after the season ended and CBS released me back to the wild. She instructed me not to return to teaching until I met with the university's high-level administration and attorneys. Beads of sweat tangoed from my armpits to the bony ends of my pelvis. Was I going to be fired? The show primarily takes place over summer vacation, so it was not like I dropped the ball on my work obligations. Before I moved into the house, I painstakingly worked with my department chair to prepare online lessons for fall class days I might miss, should I make it into latter weeks of the game. What could this meeting be about?

I had heard horror stories about so-called super fans of the program trying to get houseguests fired from their jobs. The show's 24-hour Internet feed provides opportunities for viewers to capture, isolate, and edit particularly unflattering moments and electronically send the audio and visual material, without context, to employers. Before moving into the house, I learned that a few overzealous audience members worked to have Season 6 winner Maggie Ausburn fired from her nursing job after she allegedly admitted to unsavory aspects of her past. Imagine being recorded around the clock. Nearly every word you utter is transcribed by a viewer and then posted to one of the many fan websites dedicated to *Big*

2 Investigating the Reality TV Paradox

Brother. Any dark or funny tale you tell can be ripped from its larger narrative and used as ammunition against you. This is a nightmare scenario for a queer academic with an acerbic, often inappropriate sense of humor. Would I be the next Maggie?

After listening to Amy's message, I spent a panicked-filled day preparing to convene with university administrators. I brainstormed questions they might pose and rehearsed answers. "Rehearse" carries the unflattering connotation of a ruse, as if my responses were an insincere performance designed to retain my academic post. I felt like the flawed protagonist of Gillian Flynn's novel-turned-movie *Gone Girl*, wherein a man self-consciously and uncomfortably performs the role of a husband who did not kill his wife. The character narrates how performing innocence feels inauthentic even though he is innocent of the crime.

As a performance studies scholar, I am intimately familiar with performance's deleterious associations. U.S. history is rooted in an anti-performance bias. In the late nineteenth century, Victorian Americans believed prostitutes and depraved men occupied U.S. playhouses. Members of high society condemned "the stage's use of illusionistic devices such as scenery, makeup, and costuming, all of which aimed at seducing the unwary away from reality into a false world of fantasy."[1] I use terms like "rehearse," "audience," and "performer" throughout this book in a culturally reflexive manner. I work against Puritanical traditions that view performance as immoral, unethical, and false. This project is in part a dance through murky territory that blurs lines between manipulating self-presentation and simply being.

"It's show time," I thought, as I sat in a musty university conference room across from six men in suits. A bald guy at the end of the table pulled a Dictaphone from his briefcase, pressed a button, and explained that our discussion would be recorded. Why would he have to record our conversation? Blood rushed to my face. The fast-paced, percussion-beat of my breath dizzied me. "We just have to know," one of the guys mumbled, "Why'd you do it?"

I explained that I study the ways in which gay identity is performed on stage, in mass media, and in everyday life situations. *Big Brother* provided a unique opportunity for me to position myself inside television's apparatus of production. I got a chance to be Toto from *The Wizard of Oz*. This was my chance to draw back reality TV's curtain and see how the wizard creates television magic. Involvement in the show seemed an ideal trajectory of my research agenda. "Think of all the articles about the experience I'll be able to write," I argued. "Who knows? I might even author a book about what it's like to be an academic insider *inside* reality TV."

Naïve when I signed up for the show, I earnestly believed that the university would hold viewing parties, where students and colleagues cheered me on as I competed for the half-million-dollar grand prize. It was not until I was sitting in a conference room with lawyers and administrators that I realized how much I put on the professional line when I agreed to be a houseguest. "Holy shit," I thought. "I might lose my job." If I had waited one more year, I would have at least been somewhat protected by academic tenure. But no, I had to be the bonehead who went on a reality show one year before he was awarded job security. Spoiler alert: University administrators docked my pay for the work days I missed and chastised me for not going through the appropriate administrative channels to "ok" my participation on a reality TV show; but they did not fire me.

The Ins(iders) and Out(siders) of Reality TV

Inside Reality TV offers a rare, autoethnographic, and behind-the-scenes account of my experiences on and off the set of CBS's *Big Brother*. Operating as a reality TV insider and gay academic, I reflect on the show's casting procedures, my interactions with producers, and viewer feedback. Borrowing from Media Studies critic John Corner, I investigate how

> *Big Brother* operates its claims to the real within a fully managed artificiality, in which almost everything that might be deemed to be true about what people do and say is necessarily and obviously predicated on the larger contrivance of them being there in front of the camera in the first place.[2]

Positioned inside television's representational machine, I investigate how the program's producers, fans, and players theatrically render contestants from historically marginalized groups.

In the context of reality television, sexual minorities and people of color are often reduced to stereotypes. Emphasis on character production challenges a common misconception about reality TV, namely that reality TV contestants are not actors because they "play" themselves. *Inside Reality TV* examines how reality TV producers, participants, and fans tokenize people from marginalized groups via racist, homophobic, and sexist tropes of representation. I utilize two primary research methods: autoethnography and textual analysis. I turn to autoethnography to theorize my experiences on the set of *Big Brother*. Other research methods would not provide immediate, ongoing, and *in situ* access to the *Big Brother* house, nor would CBS likely permit non-affiliated investigators to enter the show's immediate contexts, like the program's soundstage, casting interviews, and sequester house.

Second, I use spectator commentary to triangulate my autoethnographic observations and theorize how some audience members interpret gay contestants and houseguests of color. I call this method of Media Studies inquiry performative spectatorship, which is a concept I elaborate on in future chapters. Textual analysis of fan discourse illustrates how race, gender, and sexuality are interpreted and discussed by the show's viewers. The methodological act of comparing my story to viewer response helps me establish a dialogic relationship between my self-conscious enactments of identity and audience-oriented readings of other marginalized people. The book works like a mosaic in which my personal reflections, the CBS edit of the program, viewer feedback, and media theory comprise a bigger tale about how identity may be constructed on a reality show and understood by

4 Investigating the Reality TV Paradox

viewers. On a broader level, I build upon research that critiques the various ways in which people from historically oppressed groups are depicted in mass media.

Many reality TV–oriented texts, like Andrejevic's *Reality TV: The Work of Being Watched* and Biressi and Nunn's *Reality TV: Realism and Revelation*, detail the genre's history and development. In *Reality TV: Audiences and Factual Entertainment*, Annette Hill considers how reality programming exemplifies Erving Goffman's notion of everyday life performance. Grounding reality TV in performance theory is crucial given the genre's theatricality and meticulous production. Other authors opt for a more precise focus by examining gender and race on particular reality TV programs. Rachel Dubrofsky's *The Surveillance of Women on Reality Television* investigates ABC's *The Bachelor* and *The Bachelorette* and exposes strategies TV producers utilize to theatrically render gender and race. Rachel Silverman's anthology *The Fantasy of Reality* similarly concentrates on representations of race, gender, and sexuality on Bravo's *The Real Housewives* franchise. Like Dubrofsky, the authors featured in Silverman's collection do not have backstage access to the shows they critique. My opening chapter in *The Fantasy of Reality* demonstrates the limitations of this mode of critical inquiry. As an audience member, I am restricted in what I can say about *The Real Housewives*. Most viewers are not privy to conversations that take place when cameras stop rolling, nor do they witness producers prompt the cast to act a certain way, such as the time a *Big Brother* field producer requested that I deliver a bigger, more "Ragan" response to a controversial revelation. *Inside Reality TV* extends book-length intellectual considerations of reality TV offered by Andrejevic, Hill, Biressi and Nunn, Silverman and Dubrofsky by examining the concomitant relationship between *Big Brother*'s process of production and the final product that airs on CBS.

Big Brother is Watching and Watching *Big Brother*

Big Brother is one of network television's two longest-running primetime reality programs. Premiering three months after ratings juggernaut, *Survivor, Big Brother* failed to match its sister program's popularity. Media scholar Derek Foster attributes *Survivor*'s success to its competitive, win-at-all-costs format. He suggests that the program's "Outwit, Outplay, Outlast" credo serves as a "microcosm of American values."[3] *Survivor* divides its cast into two tribes and forces contestants to vote one another out of the game. "Just as in real life," Foster observes, "carefully chosen alliances and strategic friendships could bring success on *Survivor*. The brand of reality depicted on *Survivor* reinforced the widespread notion that self-interest ultimately trumps self-reliance."[4]

Big Brother, with all its Orwellian undertones, focused more on the voyeuristic aspects of reality television and downplayed competition in its premiere season. Fifty-two cameras and 95 microphones recorded ten strangers living in the *Big Brother* house. Each week, houseguests voted on two roommates for possible banishment, who then had their fate put in the audience's hands. A telephoned-in audience vote determined which of the two nominated players would be the week's evictee.

Week by week, viewers eliminated one player from the game until only two contestants remained: a 21-year-old, muscled leg-amputee named Eddie McGee and a 23-year-old former Gap model named Josh Souza. McGee and Souza embodied the very sort of elusive demographic CBS hoped to entice. Performing young, White masculinity likely played a crucial role in their ability to maintain audience favor. The night of the season finale, *BBC News* reported that, "Despite the lower-than-expected viewing figures, CBS says it has been financially successful because [*Big Brother*] attracted more young viewers, a problem for the network in the past."[5]

I became a more dedicated *Big Brother* fan during its second season when producers made the show more competition oriented. Twelve strangers moved into the house but, this time around, *Big Brother*'s audience had no say in who was eliminated, nor did they vote on the winner of the $500,000 grand prize. Houseguests now participate in weekly games to determine who has power.

A Big Brother *Crash Course*

I realize that not everyone reading this book will have seen an episode of *Big Brother*, nor will many understand the competition's rules and structure, let alone its nuance. Understanding these details, though, provides a richer appreciation for the ways in which gender, race, and sexuality are portrayed on *Big Brother*. I therefore present the following *Big Brother* crash course. I encourage you to bunny ear this page and return to it when the show's competitive structure comes into play later in the book.

The Head of Household

Each week, houseguests participate in competitions, like the Head of Household, or "HoH," contest. The first night we stepped into the *Big Brother* house, we played an HoH game titled "Hot Dog, We Have a Weiner," where production divided us into two teams. Each member of our assigned group took turns jumping on a 10-foot-tall hot dog dangling from an elevated wire. Our aim was to ride the hot dog without falling off as it traveled across the backyard to a safety zone. The first team to get all its members to the other side of the yard won. The last person across from the winning team became the season's first Head of Household.

Nominations

The victor of Thursday's HoH battle wins immunity for the week and is responsible for nominating two houseguests for eviction. A shaggy-haired, Arizona State University baseball player named Hayden was our season's first Head of

6 Investigating the Reality TV Paradox

Household. Hayden's HoH privileges included a private bedroom and bathroom, a letter from home, pictures of his loved ones, and a basket of snacks. One by one, we made our way up to Hayden's bedroom and suggested ideal candidates for our first eviction. Three days after his HoH victory, production called all 13 houseguests to the dining room, where Hayden announced names of the two people he nominated for eviction: Rachel, a red-headed cocktail waitress from Las Vegas, and Brendon, a swim instructor and doctoral student from Los Angeles. Rachel and Brendon became romantically involved only a few days into the start of the season. Romantic couplings, colloquially known as "showmances," tend to emerge every season of *Big Brother*. Showmance participants often become targets for elimination because romantic pairings represent too much influence in a game where loyalty is currency and any player securing an additional vote becomes a powerful threat.

Haves and Have-Nots

Individuals who lose Friday's Have/Have-Not game undergo food, water, and sleep restrictions for the week. Have-Nots spend downtime in their own torturous bedroom. Season 12's Have-Not room looked like a jungle prison. *Big Brother 12*'s Have-Nots slept on broken, plastic pool loungers placed next to dead bugs in glass jars. Additionally, production made our season's Have-Nots take ice-cold showers and limited our meals to a bland oatmeal-like substance called "slop."

The Power of Veto

On Saturday, six houseguests compete for the "Power of Veto," or PoV. The six PoV players include the Head of Household, the two contestants nominated for eviction, and three randomly selected houseguests. Whoever wins the PoV may nullify one of the Head of Household's nominations. If the Veto champion elects to invalidate a nomination, the HoH must name a replacement nominee. Brendon, for example, won the season's first PoV competition and took himself off the proverbial "chopping block." Brendon's decision forced Hayden to name a replacement nominee: a woman named Annie. After Monday morning's veto ceremony, each player had four days to determine which of the two nominated houseguests they would vote to evict: Rachel or Annie.

Eviction

Evictions occur during Thursday's live CBS show. Julie Chen prompts each player to enter the diary room where he or she cast an anonymous vote to evict one of the two nominated houseguests. The Head of Household and his or her two nominees are the only players who do not participate. After all the houseguests disclose their eviction vote, Julie announces the name of the eliminated player, who immediately exits the house and is no longer in contention to win the grand prize. The remaining players then enter the backyard and participate in the next Head of Household contest, which resets the competition cycle: Head of Household → Have/Have Not → Power of Veto.

Crowning the Season's Winner

The game continues until only two houseguests remain. At that point, a jury of the final seven evicted players returns to vote for which of the two remaining competitors will be crowned the season's victor.

Big Brother's Racial and Sexual Demographics

From 2000 until 2016, the *Big Brother* soundstage has provided a temporary home to 196 people. Anywhere from 9 to 17 men and women occupy the house each season. Twenty-six Black men and women, nine Asian American players, two Middle Eastern participants, 14 Latin@ houseguests, three multiracial competitors, and 20 sexual minorities partially comprise the near 200 people who have walked through *Big Brother's* front door. Since Season 2, casting director Robyn Kass and her team have brought together a diverse group of players who mirror United States' demographics. Black and Asian people, for example, maintain 12.3% and 5% of the population, respectively, and account for 13.3% and 4.6% of previous players.

Most seasons feature a few racial, ethnic, and sexual minorities embedded in a predominantly White, heterosexual, and cisgender cast. To modify Foster, shows like *Big Brother* and *Survivor* are a "microcosm of American values" insofar as they theatricalize U.S. values of self-interest and rugged individualism. "I'm not here to make friends," is the most common phrase uttered by contestants on shows like *Survivor*, *Big Brother*, *Top Chef*, *The Amazing Race*, *The Apprentice*, and *The Bachelor*. The expression encapsulates the self-serving, win-at-all-costs logic upon which U.S. capitalism and reality TV gameshows are structured.

This is not to say that producers stage and audiences interpret ruthlessness the same way, regardless of the race, sexuality, and sex of the character engendering self-interest. Take, for example, *Top Chef's* Tiffani Faison. The brassy-haired lesbian advanced to the final two of the show's premiere season. Her masculine, direct style of communication resulted in a fellow contestant labeling her a "bitch" and critics like *Entertainment Weekly's* John Vilanova describing her as the program's "first villain" who "rode her mean streak all the way to the finals of Season 1."[6] *Big Brother 3* runner-up Danielle Reyes shared Faison's fate. Reyes is widely considered to be one of *Big Brother's* all-time best strategic players, yet she lost in the final two to a significantly less calculating woman.

Competition-oriented reality programs demonstrate the ways in which self-interest is more positively connoted when the trait is associated with White,

8 Investigating the Reality TV Paradox

heterosexual men. White male self-interest is often celebrated by audience members, critics, and fellow contestants. Some of *Big Brother's* former White, male winners like Dick Donato, Will Kirby, and Mike Malin all won the game despite a degree of callousness that make Reyes's and Faison's perceived shortcomings appear innocent by comparison. Donato poured a cup of tea on a female contestant's head and spent a bulk of the season bullying houseguests from historically marginalized groups, Malin exhibited sustained misogynistic behavior in his second, prize-winning season, and Kirby credited his win to being "hated by everyone."[7] Unlike Faison and Reyes, Donato's, Malin's, and Kirby's aggressiveness, arrogance, and cruelty are coded as reasonable—charming even. Gibson and Heyse contend that hegemonic masculinity is "connected to toughness and competitiveness, the subordination of women, and the marginalization of gay men."[8] Game-based reality television programs often make the link between emotional bloodthirst, U.S. ethos, and White hegemonic masculinity explicit.

A superficial review of *Big Brother* victors demonstrates that the ability to perform heterosexuality, masculinity, and Whiteness are among the best strategies used to win. Seventeen of *Big Brother's* 19 champions are White and only one sexual minority has won. Moreover, merely six women have claimed the top prize, and a female contestant has only triumphed one time over a man when making it to the final two. Not surprisingly, reality TV producers tend to ignore unearned privileges that benefit straight, White, and male contestants but overlook structural inequity that inhibits women and sexual and racial minorities. Despite casting people from historically marginalized groups, *Big Brother's* producers often edit out the racism, sexism, and homophobia these individuals encounter while playing the game.

Throughout this book, I use the term "produced absence" to characterize situations where *Big Brother's* producers construct representational voids, such as story editors failing to address in-game homophobia and racism and casting producers denying opportunities for a gay showmance. Manufactured absence highlights silence's identity-denying protocols *and* censorship's world-producing implications. Michel Foucault's repressive hypothesis reminds us that suppression, especially as it relates to alternative sexuality, is a paradox. On one hand, repression operates as a "sentence to disappear, an injunction to silence, an affirmation of nonexistence, and, by implication, an admission that there was nothing to say about such things, nothing to see, and nothing to know."[9] On the other hand, manufactured absence becomes the very "technology of power" that "far from undergoing a process of restriction, on the contrary has been subjected to a mechanism of increasing incitement" of censored topics.[10] There is no escaping the failed mechanics of repressing non-normative sexuality. Taboo treatments of homosexuality on reality TV spark curiosity, provoke conversation, and encourage the production of discourse. Produced absence is paradoxically performative because silence, absence, and other representational voids often incite conversations about the very sexual identities they aim to annihilate.

Reality TV as a Mode of Performative Engagement

Performativity is central to this book's thesis and requires clarification within the context of television. Judith Butler uses the term "performative" to discuss the ways in which gender and sexuality are acts, or what we *do*, rather than fixed identity positions, or who we *are*. Gender "identity" is an embodied repetitive performance of interlocking gender discourses, such as television shows, print advertisements, movies, and music videos. In today's mass-mediated environment, people largely learn "appropriate" performances of gender, race, and sexuality through television programs. Borrowing from historian Daniel Boorstin's notion that "life has become stagecraft," Randall Rose and Stacy Wood suggest that TV audiences perform media consumption through a "blending of reality and mass mediated experiences that evokes life as a movie in which people play themselves."[11]

Reality television exemplifies what I call a "performative paradox." Performative paradox characterizes moments of representation that have the potential to reveal reality as a fabrication and identity as a carefully manufactured performance. In *Gender Trouble*, Butler argues that drag queens perform a similar function. "The performance of drag," she writes, "plays upon the distinction between the anatomy of the performer and the gender that is being performed. But the relation between the 'imitation' and the 'original' is, I think, more complicated."[12] She believes that drag "reveals the imitative structure of gender itself—as well as its contingency."[13] Similarly, reality television accentuates how even the most humdrum activities may be stylized and self-consciously manufactured. In Chapter 2, I focus on the paradox of "performing not-performing," or what Dubrofsky characterizes as reality TV's tendency to produce "notions of the 'natural' and 'authentic' as non-performative—spontaneous, instinctive, unrehearsed."[14]

Reality TV producers have mastered the art of staging reality and manufacturing the illusion of authenticity. Stephanie Pratt and Lauren Conrad, two stars of MTV's *The Hills*, for example, admitted their reality show was largely fiction. Producers likewise confessed to casting models and interns as friends of *The Hills'* main characters. They also disclosed that they regularly reshot critical moments that were not originally caught on camera.[15] Fans of A&E's popular reality series *Duck Dynasty* similarly learned the show does not document the real lives of the Robertson family. *The New York Times* journalist Neil Genzlinger met with the Robertson clan and discovered that:

> The episodes didn't simply follow the Robertsons around in their daily lives; the producers would often sketch out the parameters of a situation and have the family live it. What made the show work so well was that the Robertsons, fitting the Eastern elite's image of hicks, were in fact savvy media manipulators, excellent improvisers, and telegenic as heck.[16]

Matt Hoffman, one of the closest friends I made in the *Big Brother* house, had been on another reality program called *Average Joe* prior to the summer we spent together. Matt told me that *Average Joe* producers once filmed him having a conversation with a fellow cast mate. "But I wasn't talking to anyone. I was facing a tree and producers told me stuff to say," he explained.

> At one point the "average joes" were in a gymnasium. Cameras faced us and high-powered ball launchers blasted us with balls as we tried to dodge them. The "hunks" had cameras facing them, where they were hurling balls past the camera . . . at nothing. In the show that aired, it was edited to look like the guys were pegging us with the balls with some sort of superhuman strength and speed, even though we never actually played dodge ball.

I am not the first scholar to frame reality television as performative theater and simulation. Media scholars have referred to the genre as a "pornography of emotion,"[17] where feminine emotionality verifies a program's illusion of authenticity; a hybrid of game shows and soap operas;[18] and a "theatre of neoliberalism,"[19] where shows like *Big Brother* naturalize surveillance and contestants are governed by an "absolute external authority" (i.e., production) that cannot be seen or questioned. Reality television transforms even the most banal interaction into a grand production, a spectacle watched by millions. "Everyday life performance"[20] is at a heightened theatrical state on the set of *Big Brother*, where knick-knacks glued to Ikea furniture, blinding lights, dozens of cameras, microphones dangling from the ceiling, and the voices of production highlight the merge between "reality" (whatever that word means) and television.

Describing *Big Brother* as a medium of performative engagement suggests that the program is theater of the real, where reality is a consciously constructed fabrication. In this book, reality television characterizes more-or-less unscripted material produced by TV workers and told from production's perspective.[21] Having participated on a reality show, I am keenly aware that the genre does not represent reality. Authenticity, in this context, is also a construct, or set of strategies reality TV participants and producers use to create the illusion of everyday experiences. Critical media scholar Eileen Meehan reminds readers that, no matter the genre, "Television always presents an ideology for consumption to a viewership that is always and simultaneously a public celebrating meaning and an audience produced for sale in the marketplace."[22]

The Reiterative Impact of Gay Tropes on TV

Television shows repeatedly stage culturally approved methods of sexual intimacy. Think of how many times you have watched sitcoms that revolve around the delayed consummation of a primary male and female character. *Cheers'* Sam and Diane, *Moonlighting's* Maddie and David, *The Office's* Jim and Pam, *Friends'*

Ross and Rachel, and *Frasier's* Niles and Daphne are all manifestations of the same "Will they or won't they?" take on heterosexual romance. Each retelling of delayed consummation coupled by a virtual absence of gay intimacy reinforces the illusion that heterosexual sex is natural and unavoidable. TV's tales of delayed consummation—although all fundamentally the same—build upon one another and, in doing so, help establish the assumption that men and women naturally belong together and alternative sexuality should remain silent and unseen.

The stereotype that gay men are mentally ill also illustrates Butler's point. Nineteenth-century sexologists coined the term "homosexual" and placed it in a vernacular of gender inversion and mental disturbance. Michel Foucault refers to the rhetorical construction of homosexuality and its manufactured perversion as the "psychiatrization of perverse pleasure."[23] But, as Butler indicates, the sole act of naming, by itself, is not enough to create the illusion of identity. The sexologists' theory of homosexual illness had to be reiterated and cited. Television has historically greased up performative mechanisms that equate homosexuality with disease and disturbance. Media researchers invested in LGBTQ themes often refer to journalist Mike Wallace's televised documentary "The Homosexuals" to illustrate the medium's performative, world-creating power. The special aired in 1967 on CBS, the same network responsible for *Big Brother*. Fejes and Petrich note that Wallace's exposé serves as a "compilation of all the negative stereotypes of gay men (it omitted mention of lesbians)."[24] So-called expert testimony offered in "The Homosexuals" *produces* images of unbalanced, unhealthy gay men more than it *reflects* a gay man's alleged irrationality.

LGBTQ activists have long recognized television's influence on social marginalization and acceptance. Members of early homophile movements, like The National Gay Task Force, demanded that TV networks provide positive depictions of gay and lesbian people. During the 1970s, these activists instituted letter-writing campaigns protesting negative stereotypes of gay men and women on TV; they also established a successful "media project to work for change in portrayals of gays and lesbians in television."[25]

Appreciating the role reality TV has played in affirming queer standpoints requires a brief review of gay tropes that have materialized in reality television over the last 30 years. In this book, tropes refer to stock character types repeatedly depicted on television programs. Tropes represent television's reiterative, world-making capacity. Reiteration is a key theme in Butler's *Bodies that Matter*. The book's introduction includes the word in nearly every paragraph. She writes that, "Performativity is not a singular 'act,' for it is always a reiteration of norm or set of norms."[26] Butler goes on to argue that performativity gains its identity-producing power through repetition. A sophisticated analysis of racial, gender, and sexual performativity on television necessitates a careful examination of tropes, or oft-repeated modes of representation, that aim to depict people of color, women, and sexual minorities.

Prior to reality TV, gay TV characters usually fell into one of three bleak categories. First, television narratives frequently theatricalized the tale of a young

12 Investigating the Reality TV Paradox

gay person disowned—either temporarily or permanently—by friends and family members after coming out of the sexual closet. Gay self-disclosure's association with family rejection partially explains why sexual minorities in the 1980s "typically came out later in life, by which time they likely had stable jobs, adequate shelter, and financial independence."[27] Not surprisingly, the average age of coming out has become younger as media provide more affirming representations of gay people and their lives. Historical parallels between more affirming LGBTQ media visibility and increased rates of gay self-disclosure exhibit television's performative impact on performances of gay subjectivity. The Stonewall gay rights group finds that sexual minorities "over the age of 60 came out, on average, at the age of 37. People in their 30s came out when they were 21, and those aged 18–34 came out by the time they were 17."[28] Stonewall's Chief Executive Ruth Hunt reasons that people coming out of the closet at a younger age is largely due to "an explosion of role models and people talking about being gay, so [LGBTQ youth] are more able to associate what they're feeling with something they can see."[29] The rise of three-dimensional, confident, family-oriented, and community-connected LGBTQ individuals on television has provided a narrative blueprint for coming out to younger generations of sexual minorities. This was hardly the case before the 1990s, when TV relegated gay characters to stories of banishment, wrongdoing, and death.

Second, many TV dramas included the motif of gay villains determined to sabotage a program's protagonists. A gay villain's homosexuality merely added a layer to his or her multiple forms of deviance. Gay scoundrels were often depicted as psychologically unstable, sexually abusive, and so-called cross-dressers. One of the early paradoxes of initial gay representation on TV is that television writers and producers often portrayed so-called homosexual men as villains, criminals, and rapists, even though sexual minorities have historically and overwhelmingly been targets, not instigators, of crime and violence. A 1989 survey reveals that up to 92% of gays and lesbians reported they had been "targets of antigay verbal abuse or threats," and as many as 24% revealed they suffered "physical attacks because of their sexual orientation."[30] These statistics placed against ideology-driven television narratives where sexual minorities disproportionately *commit* crime underscore performativity's command over fallacious, anti-gay viewer perceptions.

Finally, stories of homosexuality often dramatized a gay man's HIV contraction and presumed eventual death. A 1987 episode of *Designing Women* ironically titled "Killing All the Right People" features a gay man dying of AIDS who hires the women of Sugarbaker & Associates to design his funeral. In the 1980s, it made sense that a homosexual TV character would be in the final throes of AIDS and obsessed with the esthetics of his funeral. Settings and character names changed with each retelling of the AIDS tale but three themes remained constant. First, gay men on 1980s TV were often HIV+. Second, gay characters were on the brink of death. Finally, gay people's HIV problem became dramatic points of crisis for a TV program's heterosexual characters. Because few television shows featured gay people in their primary cast of characters, AIDS narratives oddly detailed the impact the disease had on White, HIV-, and heterosexual people.

TV news media, on the other hand, explored AIDS in direct relation to the U.S. population most severely affected by the epidemic: gay men. Gay media historians Fred Fejes and Kevin Petrich note that:

> As the enormity and significance of the AIDS epidemic became apparent during the 1980s, the gay community became the major battle site, to which reporters flocked to get a first-hand account of the epidemic. In the process reporters and their readers were exposed to a view of gay and lesbian life very different from the 1970s hedonistic stereotypes of gay life. Editors and other media professionals began to learn more about the gay and lesbian community and thereby became sensitized to the homophobic slant of much of their previous accounts.[31]

News media offered a more compassionate look at gay men by producing human interest narratives about people infected with and affected by HIV.

Sexual Minorities and People of Color on Reality TV

TV news stories about HIV+ gay men foreshadowed an approaching wave of sympathetic sexual minorities in televised, non-fiction milieus, or a genre Annette Hill calls "popular factual television."[32] Popular factual TV includes programs ranging from crime reports and tabloid journalism to documentaries and game shows.[33] Reality TV emerged in the 1990s and blended multiple modes of factual entertainment in what Christopher Pullen describes as a "constructed reality environment."[34] Unlike its talk show and news program predecessors, reality television stimulates diegetic drama by encouraging conflict through containment.[35] A diverse cast relegated to small quarters practically guarantees soap-opera-style drama at a fraction of the production cost. Reality TV's popularity has seen a significant rise in onscreen talent from subordinated groups—men and women who have historically been under- and misrepresented in the media. But what function do sexual minorities and people of color play in the genre?

Like other reality show participants from culturally subjugated groups, I believed my involvement in *Big Brother* would enable me to "play some shared role in refashioning the mediated portrayals that have been foisted upon [sexual minorities] 'from above' by a centralized, top-down, mass medium."[36] Andrejevic and Colby maintain that the genre may appeal to sexual and racial minorities because "members of the audience—the non-media 'real' world—might be provided with the opportunity to take a part in representing themselves."[37] I quickly learned that matters of self-representation on reality TV are inhibited and facilitated by production's and the audience's perceptions of what constitutes "authentic" identity performance. Reality TV offers a theatrical arena where viewers

14 Investigating the Reality TV Paradox

witness highly stylized and meticulously edited identity performances that Alison Hearn describes as the "spectacularization of self."[38] The genre is an ideal place to study the performativity of everyday life performance because, as Hearn posits, characters on reality TV shows are "lyophilized [or freeze-dried] images of various types of 'modern individuals,' versions of the everyday self, generated inside the structural limits set by reality television show producers and editors."[39] Investigating the production of race, gender, and sexuality on *Big Brother* necessitates an overview of how people from historically marginalized groups have been performatively rendered in reality TV programming.

Sexual Minorities and the Rise of Reality Television

Pullen's suggestion that producers use gay men and people of color to catalyze confrontation first became apparent in the third season of MTV's *The Real World*. Debuting in 1994, *The Real World: San Francisco* includes a gay Cuban HIV+ man named Pedro Zamora. Pedro's life-and-death battle with AIDS becomes one of the season's principal story arcs. Producers craft a narrative where Pedro is positioned against the season's White, heterosexual villain, David "Puck" Rainey. Puck makes jokes about gay people, believes Pedro uses his disease to "play victim," dismisses his AIDS advocacy, and refuses to attend Pedro's birthday celebration. Pedro's roommates evict Puck after the AIDS educator tells them he will move out if Puck stays in the house. MTV's trailblazing, 1994 depiction of a gay Cuban man living with AIDS represents "resistance to discrimination . . . and a strong rejection of 'victim-hood status.'"[40]

Clinton-era social and economic policies helped galvanize a rising tide of gay characters on reality and scripted television. Adopting more compassionate and inclusive attitudes toward LGBTQ people helped media producers cash in on the "Dorothy dollar," or purchasing power of sexual minorities, which in the United States is estimated to be $790 billion.[41] Ron Becker points out that, "Given the circulation of discourses about gay influence in the 1990s, homosexuality fit conveniently into the delicate (and ambivalent) balance of the socially liberal, fiscally conservative agenda."[42] This is not to say that increased gay visibility on 1990s TV was exclusively profit-driven. Jon Murray, one of *The Real World's* creators, identifies as gay and "regards himself as a political agent with a personal agenda to promote gay visibility through his series."[43] Throughout the 1990s, Murray cast a diverse range of lesbian and gay cast members on the show, including *Miami's* Dan, a White model who is labeled a "flamer" by one of his roommates; *Boston's* Genesis, a White lesbian who faces anti-gay prejudice at a job site; *Seattle's* Stephen, a Black closeted man who slaps a woman in the face after she claims he is gay; *Hawaii's* Justin, a White law student who sabotages a heterosexual relationship in the house; *Hawaii's* Ruthie, a Filipina bisexual woman with substance-abuse issues; and *New Orleans's* Danny, a White man in a relationship with a closeted officer in the military.

By the summer of 2000, sexual minorities on reality television were no longer relegated to MTV. CBS's *Survivor* radically altered network TV's landscape and ushered in a new era of LGBTQ televisual representation. Gay and lesbian participants on competition-oriented reality shows offer competitive opportunities for sexual minorities to "test the equity of their skills in a mass media context."[44] Gay male participants, in particular, have used the medium to "improve public perceptions of gay men as competitors, thus undermining stereotypes that gay men are helpless, feckless, or ineffectual, particularly in confrontation with heterosexual males."[45] *Survivor*'s first champion Richard Hatch is gay and spent a significant portion of the season nude and with his genitals blurred. Hatch's cold and calculated gameplay made him the premier season's ideal villain. Fellow contestant Sue famously called Hatch a "snake" before voting for him to win the million-dollar grand prize.

Producers of reality programs like *Survivor* and *The Amazing Race* often use competition to downplay an LGBTQ contestant's same-sex attraction. The first gay champions of *The Amazing Race* illustrate how competition might obfuscate homosexuality. Well-built, masculine married couple Reichen Lehmkuhl and Chip Arndt seemingly invalidated the myth that gay men lack competitive drive and rugged, manly physiques. Lehmkuhl is a former U.S. Air Force officer and Arndt is a triathlete who likens himself to Winston Churchill. "If one were catching the show for the first time," argues Jordan Harvey, "the viewer might assume the two were friends instead of married to each other."[46] The pair's sexuality functions as a produced absence on the program. Harvey explains that,

> The show downplays the relationship between the two men, instead choosing to portray the participants as methodical and physically superior. These two men exemplify what the American culture attempts to be, except for the fact that they are gay, so their homosexuality is downplayed.[47]

Reality TV producers symbolically annihilate same-sex intimacy by 1) rarely casting two gay or two lesbian characters in the same season, 2) including two gay or lesbian characters who knew and despised one another before the show started (e.g., *Big Brother 8*'s Joe and Dustin), and 3) editing out displays of physical intimacy between sexual minorities (e.g., *Survivor: Blood vs. Water*'s Colton and Caleb).

Even reality TV programs centered around gay courtship prohibit same-sex physical encounters. Bravo's *Boy Meets Boy*, for example, marginalized gay intimacy on reality TV through 1) its performative duplication of ABC's heteronormative reality TV romance competition *The Bachelor*, and 2) the program's self-described "groundbreaking" premise that its gay bachelor is unaware his pool of suitors contains both gay and straight men. First, *Boy Meets Boy* premiered one year after ABC's popular dating gameshow *The Bachelor*. Now entering its twenty-second season, *The Bachelor* features a handsome, young, and almost always White man dating 25 women who all temporarily live in the same house. The bachelor eliminates contestants each week until only two women remain. The finale usually

16 Investigating the Reality TV Paradox

culminates in a marriage proposal offered to one of the two finalists. Similarly, *Boy Meets Boy*'s singular season starred a single, handsome, young White man named James Getzlaff. Over the course of six weeks, Getzlaff dated 15 men and eliminated romantic interests at the end of each episode. He and his final romantic interest would win $25,000 if the preferred suitor identified as gay. Selecting a heterosexual mate at the end of the game would result in no prize. The structural mechanics of *Boy Meets Boy* mirror those of *The Bachelor*, and, in turn, offer a performative and televisual enactment of homonormativity. Duggan defines homonormativity as sexual minorities enacting politics and behaviors that do not "contest dominant heteronormative assumptions and institutions but uphold and sustain them while promising the possibility of a demobilized gay constituency and a privatized, depoliticized gay culture anchored in domesticity and consumption."[48] The gay-themed show was merely a replication of ABC's exclusively heterosexual offering that plays on the heteronormative myth that "real" love must culminate in marriage—a right not enjoyed by sexual minorities in 2003.

Second, *Boy Meets Boy* dramatizes homonormative ideology by prohibiting sexual contact among its contestants. This move sharply contrasts with the sexual dynamics of *The Bachelor*, which regularly showcases heterosexual couples on sexually centered overnight dates. *Boy Meets Boy*'s no-sex clause perpetuates myths that gay sexual intimacy is somehow more salacious than sexual activity on programs like *The Bachelor*, *Joe Millionaire*, and *Paradise Hotel*, and heterosexual men are not safe around their gay counterparts. Queer media scholar Jeff Bennet argues that *Boy Meets Boy*'s "rules protected a sanitized approach to sexuality, suggesting that the men could be gay, just not sexually active on the show."[49] *Boy Meets Boy* illustrates how even reality TV programs that celebrate queer sexuality still operate under the assumption that queer sex acts are inherently dangerous and in need of correction; censorship and prohibition are merely two of the genre's corrective technologies.

The premiere of Bravo's *Queer Eye for the Straight Guy* oddly inverted the assumption that heterosexual people need to fix sexual minorities. *Queer Eye* is premised on the notion that hegemonic masculinity, not homosexuality, requires rehabilitation. *Queer Eye* positions gay men simultaneously as arbiters of appropriate heterosexual performance and the people most qualified to repair the rough-and-tumble mechanics of heteronormative manhood. In each episode, five gay men perform a makeover on a heterosexual guy. The stylists largely concentrate on making the man more palatable to his heterosexual partner.[50] Some episodes even end with a marriage proposal—an odd performative event given that, at the time of the show's run, gays and lesbians did not have the right to marry. Kelly points out that the program's preoccupation with heterosexual romance involves a "creepy case of self-ghettoization" where the self-proclaimed "Fab Five" view the reveal on monitors and in a separate location; they "literally have to watch the climax of the show from the margins."[51]

Reality TV's queer people of color contend with reductive interpretations of both their race and sexuality. *The Real World: Philadelphia*'s narrative rendering of a gay, Black man named Karamo Brown demonstrates the intersectional aspects of racism and homophobia. In one episode, police officers surround Karamo and claim they received an anonymous and incorrect tip that he had a gun. Karamo becomes understandably infuriated by the false accusation. Karamo's White roommate MJ narrates the exchange and suggests that he is overreacting, "I don't know if it's because he's gay, black or what," MJ shares in an on-camera confessional. Schroeder points out that MJ's pearl-clutching narration runs in sharp contrast to his own documented acts of aggression—incidences where his whiteness and heterosexuality are never called into question. Schroeder opines that, "The tropes of the frustrated homosexual and the angry black man create distinctions that would set any heterosexual and homosexual white male far apart from that which Karamo is constructed to embody."[52]

People of Color on Reality TV

Karamo's narrated "aggression" and assumed criminality illuminate tropes popular factual television producers utilize to portray people of color. Karamo is placed in a performative arena where racial tension is expected if not explicitly goaded by producers. Squires notes reality TV has "borrowed from broadcast television's history and techniques of integration," where one person of color is surrounded by White men and women; and the illusion of multiculturalism gives way to a "racial conflict script."[53] *The Real World*'s opening title sequence speaks to the show's quarrel-driven mechanics: "This is the true story of seven strangers picked to live in a house and have their lives taped to find out what happens when people stop being polite and start getting real." The assumption is that surveillance promotes antagonism (i.e., "stop being polite") and enables a character to reveal his or her authentic self (i.e., "start getting real").

Racial authenticity is of course strategically produced in a docu-series. In her textual analysis of representations of race on *Survivor: Cook Islands*, *Black.White.*, and *The Real World: Denver*, Bell-Jordan outlines five primary ways that race and racism are narratively brought to life on reality TV programs. She argues that the shows:

> 1) dramatize race and racial issues by juxtaposing opposing viewpoints; 2) promote conflict in the framing of race and racial issues; specifically in terms of interracial and intraracial conflict; 3) perpetuate hegemonic representations of race by emphasizing violence and anger; 4) personalize racism by privileging individual solutions to complex social problems; and 5) leave conflict and contradictions unresolved.[54]

Racial conflict and juxtaposition have been trademarks of the genre since its inception. Racial polarization is a defining characteristic of reality TV precursors like *Cops*, *LAPD: Life on the Beat*, and *World's Wildest Police Videos*. Documentary-style

18 Investigating the Reality TV Paradox

police ride-along shows disproportionately construct stories where White characters are police officers and Black and Latino men and women are criminal suspects.[55] The repeated suggestion is that White people play by the rules and people of color disrupt the peace, break laws, and are a danger to the community. Unlike *The Real World*'s and *Big Brother*'s cast, suspects featured on *Cops* and other crime-oriented reality shows do not willingly participate. Blurred-out faces and bleeped-out names indicate their surveillance is not consensual, nor is the commodification of their manufactured criminality.

Reality TV producers regularly dramatize and racialize good/evil and hero/villain binaries. In 2010 *Survivor* aired a season titled *Heroes vs. Villains*, in which 20 past contestants were invited back and split into the season's titular tribes. Only three survivors of color participated in the season. One Black man (James Clement) and one Black woman (Cirie Fields) played as heroes, and one Latina (Sandra Diaz) competed as a villain. Producers casting the season's only Black Survivors as heroes may be less progressive than the choice first appears. James and Cirie are fan favorites who both participated in three separate seasons. Hallmarks of heroism such as likability and loyalty are rarely winning traits on a show like *Survivor*. Jury members that vote on a season's winner often trumpet backstabbing and lying to rationalize their decision. Deceitfulness and betrayal are not interpreted in a positive light when performed by competitors of color. Fellow contestants often penalize Black people for "keeping it real" on *Survivor*. "Keeping it real" characterizes a propensity to call out and challenge racism and play the game in an aggressive manner. "Failure to represent a racial group 'positively,'" Drew argues, has been a "central rationale for eliminating" contestants of color.[56]

Conversely, villainous behavior tends to only be coded as an asset or positive characteristic when a competitor is a White man. The Villains tribe is composed of some of *Survivor*'s most notorious and celebrated White men, including Tyson Apostol, Rob Mariano, and Russell Hantz. The insinuation is that White villains should have multiple opportunities to display their skills but only amiable and honest Black people play multiple seasons. Of *Survivor*'s 91 returnees, ten are Black, five are Asian American, and three are Latin@. Contestants of color asked to play multiple seasons of *Survivor* (e.g., *Borneo*'s Gervase, *Redemption Island*'s Francesca, *South Pacific*'s Ozzy, and *Fiji*'s Yau-Man) are overwhelmingly good-humored, trustworthy, and honorable to a fault. By inviting back a certain type of contestant from a racially marginalized group, *Survivor*'s production team engages in a rhetoric of tokenism through which the token must be "exceptional, and their exceptionalism 'bolsters the premises of meritocracy and individualism'" celebrated on the show.[57] Cloud argues that tokens are not present "only by virtue of their race or gender; indeed, representatives of oppressed groups often must be *more* qualified and hardworking than members of dominant groups in the same position."[58] In the context of *Survivor*, contestants of color will be invited back if they somehow managed to advance to the latter stages of the game using heroic strategies that *rarely* result in success. Interestingly, neither James nor Cirie advanced to the midpoint of *Heroes vs. Villains*, but Sandra, the Villain tribe's only contestant of color, won *Heroes vs. Villains* and became the first and only person to win multiple seasons of *Survivor*.

Reality TV has largely "reinforced existing racialized mass-mediated caricatures."[59] Boylorn notes that Black women on television tend to

> fall into historical categories and stereotypes that range from the hypersexual Jezebel to the asexual Mammy and contemporary versions of each. Other negative images include sluts, divas, hoochies, weepers, waifs, whores, antagonizers, shrills, welfare queens, freaks and hot mammas.[60]

Critical media scholars provide numerous examples of Black caricatures on reality TV, such as *Road Rules'* use of "ghetto signifiers" to authenticate the blackness of a participant named Gladys;[61] *Flavor of Love*'s depiction of "ghetto girl" and "pimp" stereotypes;[62] and *The Real World's* tendency to pit the "angry Black man" and the "reasonable Black man" against one another.[63] Tyree's thematic analysis of ten reality shows reveals other emergent stereotypes of Black men and women, such as the Oreo, or Black person who "acts White" (e.g., *College Hill's* Jon); homo thug, or gay person who embodies "thug" masculinity (e.g., *The Real World: Philadelphia's* Karamo); and coon or clown (e.g., *Strange Love's* Flavor Flav).[64]

Media scholars have also celebrated the medium's potential to include people of color, avoid racial stereotypes, and present three-dimensional depictions of Black subjects. In her critical analysis of *Run's House* and *Snoop Dogg's Fatherhood*, Smith explores how Black fathers are shown as present in the home, even-keeled disciplinarians, and positive role models to their children.[65] Similarly, Black women on *The Real Housewives of Atlanta* have used the show as an arena to showcase their entrepreneurial talents. NeNe Leakes' memorable one-liners, larger-than-life personality, acting skills, and gift for self-promotion have resulted in guest spots on local newscasts, a recurring stint on Fox's *Glee*, a hosting job on E! Network's *Fashion Police*, and a supporting role on NBC's *The New Normal*.[66] Several of *Atlanta's* cast members use the show to promote their businesses. Cynthia Bailey, Lisa Wu, and Sheree Whitfield promote their respective retail lines, Kandi Burruss markets her musical endeavors, and producers advertise Kenya Moore's and Phaedra Parks' workout videos. NeNe, Cynthia, Kandi, and their *Real Housewives of Atlanta* co-stars succeed in business by using reality TV to brand the self and cultivate parasocial relationships with viewers/consumers. Buying Cynthia's eyewear or Kenya's exercise DVD enables audience members to feel as if they are engaged in a reciprocal relationship with the women. Self-described "super fans" demonstrate their support for a character by purchasing the TV personality's products.

"Super Fans" and Performative Spectatorship

Over the last 17 years, *Big Brother* has amassed a loyal, passionately engaged group of fans. Casual viewers watch the CBS broadcast of *Big Brother* three times a week. The "super fan" label is reserved for men and women who spend a significant part of their summers glued to *Big Brother's* 24-hour live Internet feed. Many super fans use Internet forums to debate about the season's characters and developments. One of the most popular Web sites dedicated to *Big Brother* fan discussion is SurvivorSucks.com.

The *Big Brother* forum on the *Survivor Sucks* Web site contains 1,025,859 posts about the show and daily recaps in which alternating members author textual representations of the program's 24-hour Internet feed. These fans create secondary texts that function intertextually to favor selected readings of a primary text, like *Big Brother*. Throughout this book, I emphasize unique ways that audience members play a meaningful role in constructing characters and narratives they view on television.

Televisual reception, in other words, may also be framed as an act of production. I use the term "performative spectatorship" to theorize how audience members aid in the rhetorical and theatrical construction of sexual minorities and people of color. Racist, sexist, and homophobic stereotypes constrain and enable the ways in which viewers interpret gay characters, women, and people of color. *Big Brother's* production team helps facilitate this process by using music, narration, and other editing devices to underscore certain character motifs, like the angry Black woman and crying gay man. These tropes are entrenched and reproduced, even when participants actively work to resist them.

Chapter 3 of *Inside Reality TV* focuses on how *Big Brother's* production team, cast members, and viewers rely on stereotypical modes of gay representation when performatively rendering and interpreting gay and lesbian characters. I specifically theorize the performative construction of my gay identity in the immediate context of the show. My reflections include "insider" knowledge normally edited out of aired episodes, such as conversations between production and cast members. While many media and performance scholars have written about reality television, few if any have been uniquely positioned backstage (auditions and meetings with producers) and on stage (onscreen talent) while collecting data.

In Chapter 4, I turn my attention to the ways in which production and audience members engage in performative spectatorship to manufacture race on *Big Brother*. Performativity is typically theorized as a method of enactment. My investigation of racist and sexist audience commentary enables me to elaborate on the relationship between audience-constructed texts (e.g., fan commentary) and primary texts (e.g., *Big Brother*). Suggesting fan involvement functions as a form of textual production radically challenges an arbitrary binary that positions television producers as message senders and television viewers as relatively passive receivers of mediated communication.

The concluding chapter offers final ruminations on my experiences as a former (and recovering) *Big Brother* houseguest. Reflecting on the 2007–2008 Writers Guild of America Strike, I consider how reality shows like *Big Brother* function as a neoliberal matrix of power. I also discuss the importance of audience-text intertextuality as it relates to reality TV.

Notes

1 John S. Gentile, *Cast of One: One-person Shows from the Chautauqua Platform to the Broadway Stage* (Chicago: University of Illinois Press, 1989), 5.
2 John Corner, "Performing the Real: Documentary Diversions," *Television and News Media* 3, no. 3 (2002): 256.
3 Derek Foster, "'Jump in the Pool': The Competitive Culture of *Survivor* Fan Networks," *Understanding Reality Television*, ed. Su Holmes and Deborah Jermyn (New York, NY: Routledge, 2004), 279.
4 Ibid., 280.
5 BBC News. "Eddie Wins Big in *Big Brother*," last modified September 30, 2000, accessed January 12, 2017, http://news.bbc.co.uk/2/hi/entertainment/949910.stm.
6 John Villanova, "*Top Chef Duels* Recap: 'Tiffani Fiason vs. Dale Talde," *Entertainment Weekly*, last modified September 11, 2014, accessed October 6, 2017, http://ew.com/recap/top-chef-duels-season-1-episode-6.
7 Josh Wok, "EW.com Meets the Winner of *Big Brother 2*," *Entertainment Weekly*, last modified September 26, 2001, accessed October 6, 2017, http://ew.com/article/2001/09/26/ewcom-meets-winner-big-brother-2.
8 Katie L. Gibson and Amy L. Heyse, "The Difference Between a Hockey Mom and a Pit Bull': Sarah Palin's Faux Maternal Persona and Performance of Hegemonic Masculinity at the 2008 Republican National Convention," *Communication Quarterly* 58, no. 3 (2010): 236–7.
9 Michel Foucault, *The History of Sexuality, Volume 1: An Introduction*, trans. Robert Hurley (New York, NY: Vintage, 1978), 4.
10 Michel Foucault, *The History of Sexuality, Volume 1: An Introduction*, 12.
11 Randall L. Rose and Stacy L. Wood, "Paradox and the Consumption of Authenticity Through Reality Television," *Journal of Consumer Research* 32, no. 2 (2005): 284.
12 Judith Butler, *Gender Trouble: Feminism and the Subversion of Identity* (New York, NY: Routledge, 1990), 187.
13 Ibid.
14 Rachel E. Dubrofsky, "Fallen Women in Reality TV: A Pornography of Emotion," *Feminist Media Studies* 9 (2009): 396.
15 Noelle Devoe, "*Laguna Beach*" and "*The Hills*" Producers Finally Reveal What was Real and What Was Fake, *Seventeen*, last modified June 1, 2016, accessed February 10, 2016, www.seventeen.com/celebrity/movies-tv/news/a40784/laguna-beach-the-hills-producers-finally-reveal-what-was-real-and-what-was-fake/
16 Neil Genzlinger, "*Duck Dynasty* Legacy, Real, Fake and Upfront About It," *The New York Times*, last modified November 17, 2016, accessed February 10, 2016, www.nytimes.com/2016/11/18/arts/television/duck-dynasty-legacy-real-fake-and-upfront-about-it.html?_r=0.
17 Rachel E. Dubrofsky, "Fallen Women in Reality TV," 353–68.
18 Stephen Tropiano, "Playing It Straight: Reality Dating Shows and the Construction of Heterosexuality," *Journal of Popular Film and Television* 37, no. 2 (2009): 56–63.
19 Nick Couldry, "Reality TV, or the Secret Theater of Neoliberalism," *Review of Education, Pedagogy, and Cultural Studies* 20, no. 1 (2008): 3–13.
20 Erving Goffman, *The Presentation of Self in Everyday Life* (Woodstock: Overlook, 1973), 73.
21 Su Holmes and Deborah Jermyn, "Introduction: Understanding Reality TV," *Understanding Reality Television* (New York, NY: Routledge, 2004), 1–32.
22 Eileen R. Meehan, "Conceptualization Culture as Commodity: The Problem of Television," *Critical Studies in Mass Communication* 3 (1986): 449.
23 Michel Foucault, *The History of Sexuality, Volume 1: An Introduction*, 105.
24 Fred Fejes and Kevin Petrich, "Invisibility, Homophobia and Heterosexism," 400.
25 Fred Fejes and Kevin Petrich, "Invisibility, Homophobia and Heterosexism: Lesbians, Gays and the Media," *Critical Studies in Media Communication* 10, no. 4 (1993): 400.

22 Investigating the Reality TV Paradox

26 Judith Butler, *Bodies that Matter: On the Limits of 'Sex'* (New York, NY: Routledge, 1993), xxi.

27 David Wagner, "Nowhere to Go: Issue Brief on Gay and Transgender Youth Homelessness," *Center for American Progress*, last modified August 10, 2010, accessed January 28, 2017, www.americanprogress.org/issues/lgbt/reports/2010/08/10/8224/nowhere-to-go.

28 "Poll: Gay People Coming Out Earlier," *Advocate*, last modified November 15, 2010, accessed January 28, 2017, www.advocate.com/news/daily-news/2010/11/15/poll-gay-people-coming-out-earlier.

29 Ibid.

30 Gregory Herek, "Hate Crimes Against Lesbians and Gay Men: Issues for Research and Policy," *American Psychologist* 44, no, 6 (1989): 948.

31 Ibid.

32 Annette Hill, *Reality TV: Audiences and Popular Factual Television* (New York, NY: Routledge, 2005).

33 Ibid., 14.

34 Christopher Pullen, "The Household, the Basement and The Real World: Gay Identity in the Constructed Reality Environment," *Understanding Reality Television*, ed. Su Holmes and Deborah Jermyn (New York, NY: Routledge, 2004), 212.

35 Ibid., 215.

36 Mark Andrejevic and Dean Colby, "Racism and Reality TV: The Case of MTV's Road Rules," *How Real Is Reality TV? Essays on Representation and Truth* (Jefferson, NC: McFarland and Company, 2006), 196.

37 Ibid.

38 Alison Hearn, "'John, a 20-Year-Old Boston Native with a Great Sense of Humor': ON the Spectacularization of the 'Self' and the Incorporation of Identity in the Age of Reality Television," *International Journal of Media and Cultural Politics* 2, no. 2 (2006): 133.

39 Ibid., 137.

40 Simon Watney, *Imagine Hope: AIDS and Gay Identity* (London: Routledge, 2000), 261.

41 "LBGT Buying Power Equals $790 Billion," Wisconsin Gazette, accessed November 5, 2013, www.wisconsingazette.com/breaking-news/lgbt-buying-power-equals-790-billion.html.

42 Ron Becker, *Gay TV and Straight America* (New Brunswick: Rutgers University Press, 2006), 130.

43 Christopher Pullen, "Gay Performativity and Reality Television: Alliances, Competition, and Discourse," *The New Queer Aesthetic on Television: Essays on Recent Programming*, ed. James R. Keller and Leslie Stratyner (Jefferson, NC: McFarland and Company, 2006), 163.

44 Ibid., 165.

45 Ibid.

46 Jordan Harvey "The Amazing 'Race': Discovering a True American," *How Real Is Reality TV: Essays on Representation and Truth*, ed. David S. Escoffery (Jefferson, NC: McFarland and Company, 2006), 224.

47 Ibid.

48 Lisa Duggan, "The New Homonormativity: The Sexual Politics of Neoliberalism," *Materializing Democracy: Toward a Revitalized Cultural Politics*, ed. Dana D. Nelson and Russ Castronovo (Durham, NC: Duke University Press, 2002), 179.

49 Jeffrey A. Bennett, "In Defense of Gaydar: Reality Television and the Politics of the Glance," *Critical Studies in Media Communication* 23, no. 5 (2006): 418.

50 Katherine Sender, "Queens for a Day: Queer Eye for the Straight Guy and the Neoliberal Project," *Critical Studies in Media Communication* 23, no. 2 (2006): 146.

51 Christopher Kelly, "Gay TV Comes Out, but Who's Proud?" *Fort Work Star-Telegram*, September 8, 2003.
52 Elizabeth R. Schroeder, "'Sexual Racism' and Reality Television: Privileging the White Male Prerogative on MTV's The Real World," *How Real Is Reality TV: Essays on Representation and Truth*, ed. David S. Escoffery (Jefferson, NC: McFarland and Company, 2006), 188.
53 Catherine R. Squires, "The Conundrum of Race and Reality Television," *A Companion to Reality Television*, ed. Laurie Ouellette (Malden, MA: Wiley Blackwell, 2017), 268.
54 Katrina E. Bell-Jordan, "Black. White. and a Survivor of the Real World: Constructions of Race on Reality TV," *Critical Studies in Media Communication* 25, no. 4 (2008): 357.
55 Mary Beth Oliver, "Portrayals of Crime, Race, and Aggression in 'Reality-Based Police Shows: A Content Analysis," *Journal of Broadcasting and Electronic Media* 38, no. 2 (1994): 179–92.
56 Emily M. Drew, "Pretending to Be 'Postracial': The Spectacularization of Race and Reality TV's Survivor," *Television and New Media* 12, no. 4 (2011): 333.
57 Dana L. Cloud, "Hegemony or Concordance? The Rhetoric of Tokenism in 'Oprah' Winfrey's Rags-to-Riches Biography," *Critical Studies in Media Communication* 13, no. 2 (1996): 123; Judith Long Laws, "The Pscyhology of Tokenism," *Sex Roles* 1, no. 1 (1975): 51.
58 Dana L. Cloud, "Hegemony or Concordance," 123.
59 Mark Orbe, "Representations of Race in Reality TV: Watch and Discuss," *Critical Studies in Media Communication* 25, no. 4 (2008): 350.
60 Robin M. Boylorn, "As Seen on TV: An Autoethnographic Reflection on Race and Reality Television," *Critical Studies in Media Communication* 25, no. 4 (2008): 417.
61 Mark Andrejevic and Dean Colby, "Racism and Reality TV: The Case of MTV's Road Rules," 195–211.
62 Rachel E. Dubrofsky and Antoine Hardy, "Performing Race in Flavor of Love and The Bachelor," *Critical Studies in Media Communication* 25, no. 4 (2008): 373–92.
63 Catherin Squires, "Race and Reality TV: Tryin' to Make It Real—but Real Compared to What?" *Critical Studies in Media Communication* 25, no. 4 (2008): 436.
64 Tia Tyree, "African American Stereotypes in Reality Television," *Howard Journal of Communications* 22 (2011): 394–413.
65 Debra C. Smith, "Critiquing Reality-Based Televisual Black Fatherhood: A Critical Analysis of Run's House and Snoop Dogg's Father Hood," *Critical Studies in Media Communication* 25, no. 4 (2008): 393–412.
66 Ragan Fox, "Queering Housewives," *The Fantasy of Reality: Critical Essays on 'The Real Housewives'*, ed. Rachel E. Silverman (New York, NY: Peter Lang, 2015), 23.

2

"JUST BE YOURSELF," AND OTHER CASTING FAIRY TALES

Scholarly critiques of reality television focus almost exclusively on behavior that takes place in slickly produced network broadcasts. Most media studies researchers lack behind-the-scenes access to the programs they study. The significance of this constraint cannot be overstated. Reality show producers tirelessly work to conceal the ways in which they manufacture so-called reality. Feminist media scholars Sarah Banet-Weiser and Laura Portwood-Stacer point out that reality television workers "hide the constructed nature of the programme and thus present the subjects of the programme as eminently authentic and genuine."[1] *Big Brother*'s producers, for instance, mandated that we never talk about production. "The show isn't about us," they explain to contestants. "It's about you." But producers play a pivotal role in crafting a reality TV show's narratives and characters. A nuanced critique of the genre must account for production's machinations. In this chapter, I consider how *Big Brother*'s audition process helps construct the program's illusions of reality and authenticity.

I use the term "performance" in relation to production to figuratively describe the backstage contrivances of reality television. In *The Presentation of Self in Everyday Life*, sociologist Erving Goffman uses theater as a metaphor to understand human interaction in workplace settings. Like actors in a play, people perform characters that are determined by context and audience. Theorists have used Goffman's dramaturgical model of communication to study a dizzying range of everyday-life performance, including behavior in public restrooms,[2] stigma-management rehearsal among Muslim American youth,[3] doctor-nurse impression management in hospital wards,[4] and performances that take place between pets and their owners.[5]

Goffman's distinction between frontstage and backstage performance provides a fitting way to theorize different behaviors that emerge on and off *Big Brother*'s cameras. Frontstage is marked by a performer's "continuous presence before a particular set of observers."[6] Each week, *Big Brother*'s producers edit 168 hours of footage down to roughly two-and-a-half hours of televised content. Network broadcasts comprise a reality show's frontstage performance. But, as Goffman points out, "the vital secrets of a show are visible backstage,"[7] where people rehearse and sometimes set aside their frontstage personae. Ethnography is one of the only research methods that can peek behind reality TV's theatrical curtain. As an autoethnographer, I am uniquely positioned to reveal how "the whole machinery of self-production is cumbersome and sometimes breaks down, exposing its separate components: back region control; team collusion; audience tact; and so forth."[8]

Backstage is where we see people transform into characters. In the theater, a backstage view allows us to witness a middle-aged woman applying makeup to appear 20 years older. She is taught the proper methods of makeup application and is instructed to wear a particular costume. In academia, a backstage glance might reveal all the work a professor puts into crafting and refining a joke used in lecture. The joke should be within the limits of good taste and should be a natural extension of course content. Certain backstage rules authorize the actor's and professor's respective performances of self. Eve Sedgwick uses the term "peri-performativity" to theorize communicative mechanisms that facilitate the *doing* of identity.[9] A peri-performative understanding of identity examines rules that govern what may be spoken in a speech setting. The U.S. Supreme Court's Clear and Present Danger doctrine illustrates Sedgwick's point. Free speech in the United States may be curtailed if it presents a clear and present danger to citizens. A classic example of the doctrine is that one may not yell "Fire!" in a crowded theater if there is not in fact a fire. The Clear and Present Danger doctrine functions as a peri-performative because the rule dictates the conditions of speech. Performative interpretations of identity must consider the peri-performative aspects of speech, or the rules and customs that dictate what may or may not be uttered in a given context.

Two examples from *Big Brother* illustrate the peri-performative dynamics of self-presentation. First, contestants sign a contract with CBS that prohibits them from writing about show-related experiences for three years (see Figure 2.1). The agreement literally restricts a houseguest's speech and forbids sharing information about show participation. Conversely, the contract requires contestants to:

> irrevocably grant and release to Producer, in perpetuity and throughout the universe, the exclusive right to depict, portray and represent me and my life and all episodes, exploits, events, incidents, situations, and experiences . . . related to my life which occur, will occur or have occurred at any time.

CBS's contractual shorthand for the peri-performative control they claim over a houseguest's narrative portrayal is fittingly called "Life Story."

CONFIDENTIALITY AND LIFE STORY RIGHTS

50. (a) I understand any appearance I may make on the Series is strictly for the purpose of participating in the Series as a participant. Except as specifically provided herein or as otherwise authorized by Producer and Network, I will not myself, and I will not authorize others to, publicize, advertise or promote my appearance on the Series, receive or generate any monetary advantage from my appearance on the Series, or use or disclose to any party any information or trade secrets obtained or learned as a result of my participation in the Series, including, without limitation, any information concerning or relating to the Series, the participants, the events contained in the Series or the outcome of the Series (collectively, "Confidential Information"), for a period from the date of this Applicant Agreement until three (3) years after the initial broadcast of the last episode of the Series (i.e., the last episode of the Series as a whole, as distinct from the Episode Cycle in which I may be included as a participant or selected as an alternate). Without limiting the foregoing, I acknowledge that the initial broadcast of the Episode Cycle in which I may participate may occur, if at all, after the occurrence of the events depicted in the episodes and that any information revealed or disclosed prior to broadcast of the applicable episode will cause irreparable harm to Producer and Network. In that connection, I specifically agree that any Confidential Information, which shall include, without limitation, any information regarding the events portrayed in any particular episode, any other events occurring in or around the House, the elimination of participants and the selection of any winner, is to be held in strict confidence by me and cannot be disclosed by me to any third parties. Without limiting the foregoing in any way, I will not myself, and I will not authorize others to, prepare or assist in the preparation of any written work, any audio work, visual work or any audio-visual work that depicts, concerns, or relates in any way to my appearance on the Series or my application to appear on the Series. During the Exclusive Period (as defined in paragraph 2 of this Applicant Agreement, and as it may be extended by the Option described in paragraph 2), all contact with the media regarding the Series or my participation in the Series must be organized and sanctioned by the press officer of Producer or Network in connection with the Series or by a duly authorized representative of the Producer or Network. I acknowledge and agree that I have previously executed and delivered to Producer a confidentiality agreement in connection with my application and possible participation in the Series and all terms and conditions in such confidentiality agreement shall be incorporated and made a part of this Applicant Agreement by this reference. I agree that disclosure by me in violation of the foregoing shall constitute and be treated as a material breach of this Applicant Agreement which will cause irreparable harm to Producer and/or Network

FIGURE 2.1   Page 17 of *Big Brother*'s Applicant Agreement

"Just Be Yourself"   **27**

Second, casting only one gay person each season limits a sexual minority's opportunities to perform intimacy. Without a love interest, gay characters on reality TV are rendered symbolically impotent. They can disclose their sexual preference but the peri-performative constraints of *Big Brother* never allow them to performatively enact desire. Foucault might refer to peri-performativity as one of the many "games of truth" that manufacture and mediate reality and identity. Foucault's gaming metaphor proves especially fitting for my critical, autoethnographic account of *Big Brother* because "players in a game of truth—as opposed to powerless spectators—participate by learning to think differently, repeatedly seeking an outside to the existing confines of the game."[10]

This book represents one way I have reclaimed my presentation of self from CBS. Reclamation requires a sophisticated, self-reflexive consideration of how I transitioned from a *Big Brother* viewer to a character on the show. The casting process provides the most revealing and heuristically provocative look at how reality show participants are molded into stock characters. Casting, after all, is where reality TV's peri-performative foundation is constructed.

Being there.[11] March 27, 2010

My old neighbor Vivicca calls my cell as I drive down Santa Monica Boulevard. "Guess where I am? I'm at an open call audition for *Big Brother*. You should come," Vi proposes.

"I don't know. I drank way too much last night. I look like hell. I'm in no mood to stand in a long line only to get rejected by some cheesy casting producer."

"The audition is in the neighborhood," she coaxes. "I'm at a building on La Cienega between Santa Monica and Melrose."

My car rolls up to the Santa Monica and La Cienega intersection as Vi announces the location of the casting call. "What are the odds?" I think. I am at a crossroads. Literally. I can continue down Santa Monica Boulevard and go home or make a right turn, drive half a block, and attend my first Hollywood audition. I make a last-second right turn on La Cienega and drive to the audition.

Roughly 60 people stand in a line that snakes around a shuttered nightclub. Vi has already been waiting an hour to see *Big Brother* casting producers, so she is already inside the building when I finally enter the fray. A beautiful Asian woman stands behind me. Long, dark mane falls in near-perfect cascades over her sun dress. She looks like she is auditioning for a pop-music video. "How many of these have you attended?" she inquires.

"This is my first," I confess. "How about you?"

"I go to shit like this *all* the time. I auditioned for *The Amazing Race* last week," she announces between pops of sweet-smelling gum.

Other people waiting to audition look ridiculous. A middle-aged, Black woman in an ill-fitted red leotard steps out of line every so often and performs

28 "Just Be Yourself"

amateur acrobatics. At 2:13 p.m., she does a cartwheel. At 2:25, she rolls on the ground in a move that approximates a somersault. Looking down at my plain gray t-shirt and Gap jeans, I feel painfully ordinary. Where is my gimmick? Where is my red leotard?

Thirty minutes into my wait, houseguests from previous seasons walk out of the club and start conversations with *Big Brother*'s latest batch of hopefuls. "Evel! Evel!" a fan bellows. "Evel! Over here." Evel is a reference to the winner of *Big Brother*'s eighth season: Dick Donato. "Evel" is Dick's sobriquet and a nickname that fits his weathered appearance. Dick sports dyed black, spikey hair and a soul patch. Faded tattoos wrap up his 47-year-old arms, like ivy clinging to a decayed building. Before his stint on *Big Brother*, Dick was allegedly Keith Richards' stand-in for the motion picture *Pirates of the Caribbean: At World's End*. When I describe Dick as "weathered," remember that it takes a certain *je ne sais quoi* to qualify as *Keith Richards'* pirate stand-in.

Other *Big Brother* hopefuls plead for Dick's attention, creating a chorus of men and women chanting, "Evel! Evel!" Dick rubs his hands together, grins, and grows increasingly animated as he talks to the people surrounding him. Dick loves attention, good or bad. During his season, he spit thick balls of phlegm all over the backyard, performed yellow-face stereotypes of Asian people, burned a woman with a cigarette and poured iced tea over her head, and repeatedly referred to a gay contestant as "princess." CBS did not include most of Dick's more repellant moments in its broadcasts. I only learned about the worst of his in-game comportment by visiting fan sites that provide verbatim quotations from *Big Brother*'s Internet feed. In one transcribed rant, Dick tells a fellow houseguest that, "All the gay guys in West Hollywood used to go around and say, 'I'm clean, I don't have HIV,' when they weren't."[12] *Today Show* contributor Andy Denhart describes Dick as "the worst of a group of horrible people" featured in Season 8. "The tragic part," Denhart continues, "is something about the structure of *Big Brother*'s game keeps giving the worst of the worst the prize."[13]

Denhart's reference to a tragic and ambiguous "something" needs clarification. "Some/*thing* about the structure of *Big Brother*" is the *same thing* that benefits people like Dick outside the house. "Some/*thing* about the structure of *Big Brother*" is also the *same thing* that works against people of color, sexual minorities, and women. Of the show's 17 champions, Dick is 1 of 16 Caucasian people, 1 of 16 heterosexual men and women, and 1 of 12 men to claim the show's top prize. CBS opting to leave Dick's homophobic, sexist, and racist behaviors on the cutting-room floor mirrors more widespread institutional silence regarding homophobia, sexism, and racism.

Sticky sweat drips down my torso. "What am I doing here?" I think. On two separate occasions, I nearly leave the line and go home. Home! I can set camp under my wall-unit A/C and sleep away my hangover. An internal dialogue plays out in my head. One voice tells me that I am wasting my time. Another voice reasons, "You've already spent an hour in line. You're almost in the door."

"Just Be Yourself" **29**

Curiosity rules the day. A young, curly-haired woman named Katrina★[14] swings open the doors and ushers me into the building. She assigns me number 163 and then pulls the Polaroid camera hanging around her neck to her eyes. Katrina takes my photo and instructs me to fill out a half-sheet of paper. I scribble my name, phone number, job, and date of birth and wait for somebody to call the number Katrina assigned me.

Twenty minutes later, Katrina bounces back to the bar area and asks 162, 163, 164, and 165 to follow her to the next room. Three other men and I walk to a banquette located in the bar's patio. A 30-something, White guy and two perky, young White women greet us. The casting producers ask each of us what we do for a living and why we want to be on *Big Brother*. One man in my group is a mortician who recently lost his wife in a car accident. *Big Brother* regularly casts men and women with interesting, off-beat jobs. Previous seasons include an FBI agent, neuroscientist, and gay cowboy. The guy next to me is a likable mortician. The casting agents must be salivating.

The man at the banquette turns his attention my way. A half-smile grips the right side of his face when he discovers I am a professor. He asks about my area of expertise.

"Communication," I answer. That sounds boring. "I analyze the way people interact. Communication includes a range of study, from pinpointing nonverbal cues that indicate a lie to teaching students how to deliver killer public speeches." I still sound and look unexciting, the utter antithesis of a woman in a crimson leotard, a widower mortician, and Keith Richards' stand-in for a big-budget movie. The auditioners thank us for applying and ask us to leave through the fire exit to our immediate right.

An hour later, I am relaxing at home when a representative from Kassting, Inc. calls to invite me to a semifinal audition that will take place tomorrow. The man on the other end of the line tells me to drive to a Studio City hotel at 3:30 p.m. with a filled-out application. He insists that I keep the audition a secret from friends and family. After we end our call, I visit the *Big Brother* website, where I download a copy of the 13-page application. The form's 70 questions are split into four sections: The Basics, Family & Lifestyle, Medical & Psychological, and Your Chance to be Creative. Some of the questions require little thought, such as, "(9) What school(s)/college(s)/university(ies) have you attended/are you attending? If you're currently a student, tell us about your major(s) or course of study." Other queries are more philosophical, like, "(27) What are your thoughts on religion?" A few topics come out of left field, such as, "(58) Have you ever been to a nude beach? If so, what was it like?" It takes me two hours to complete the application. The day's excitement has drained my energy. I hop into bed and dream of life in the *Big Brother* house.

The next day, I drive to a hotel in the valley. The San Fernando Valley is home to many of Hollywood's movie and television studios. Casting producers sent me an email last night. Their message instructs me to go to the second floor of the

30 "Just Be Yourself"

hotel. The email's author warns, "You CANNOT tell anyone at your interview location that you are there for *Big Brother*. Don't approach the hotel staff regarding your interview. The hotel does NOT know that *Big Brother* is casting there." I am assigned number six at the semifinal audition. "Wow, six is my lucky number," I exclaim. A casting agent takes more Polaroid shots of me. I perform a more gregarious version of myself than I did yesterday. My mouth opens wide for a toothy, exaggerated smile. She mentions that she loves my suspenders. Yes, I even spent time deliberating over my outfit, opting for a white V-neck, jeans, and thin, hipster black suspenders.

Forty minutes later, I sit in a conference room with a pretty blonde woman named Aubrey★. She tells me the interview will last about 15 minutes, then pushes record on a video camera placed between the two of us. Aubrey commands me to look at her, and not the camera and encourages me to be myself. I answer a series of open-ended questions about my life and desire to be a contestant on *Big Brother*. If our conversation had a table of contents, it would look something like this:

Table of Contents

Part 1   Childhood

> Chapter 1   Mom and dad split when I was an infant.
> Chapter 2   Dad raised me.
> Chapter 3   Bullied in school.

Part 2   I Am the Very Model of a Modern Homosexual

> Chapter 4   Coming out of the closet at 18. Dad's abandonment.
> Chapter 5   My queer journey through academia.
> Chapter 6   Looking for love in all the wrong places.

Aubrey arches a well-plucked eyebrow when she learns I do not have a boyfriend. I joke, "I am terminally single. If being single were cancer, I'd be in Phase 4." She giggles. "My sister Tina thinks I have abandonment issues. My mother divorced my father when I was an infant and my father died six years ago." I notice the casting agent quickly send a text message on her phone. Five minutes later, another woman enters the room and sits next to Aubrey. We are now 35 minutes into what was supposed to be a 15-minute interview. The topic has somehow shifted to my workout regimen. "I work out five times a week. When I moved to Los Angeles, I was a smoker who weighed 118 pounds. That shit doesn't fly when you're a gay in LA. I quit smoking three years ago, hit the gym, and put on twenty-five pounds of muscle. Want to see?" The women enthusiastically nod their heads. I pull my shirt off and we all laugh at the moment's fitting absurdity. I leave the audition ten minutes after my chest reveal. Did I just nail my *Big Brother* audition?

A Phenomenological Critique of Authenticity

Being here

I waited two months before a woman named Samantha★ from Kassting, Inc. called to tell me I advanced to the final round of auditions. Samantha explained that I would be at a hotel next to Los Angeles's iconic LAX airport anywhere from one day to a week. She also pleaded with me to keep my involvement a secret. Producers would disqualify me if they discovered I told others I made it to the final round.

I began preparing for finals the moment my call with Samantha ended. A lot of work goes into performing self when auditioning for a reality show. I had to pick out a week's worth of clothing, anticipate questions they might ask, and prepare great autobiographical stories to share. I am not a concise storyteller, so I rehearsed various personal narratives and tried to whittle them down to brief but revealing anecdotes. The trick was to avoid sounding rehearsed in my interviews. My tales should appear off-the-cuff and my storytelling skills should seem effortless. This sort of preparation exemplifies the paradox of "performing not-performing," or what Dubrofsky characterizes as reality TV's tendency to produce "notions of the 'natural' and 'authentic' as non-performative—spontaneous, instinctive, unrehearsed."[15]

Casting producers encouraging potential houseguests to "be themselves" play into the performing not-performing paradox. Robyn Kass' team seeks extroverts but has little interest in women in red leotards performing amateur acrobatics to get attention. They look for an interesting character whose performance of authenticity is convincing enough to make the television audience ignore an array of reality TV contrivances, like production playing background music to amplify humorous and dramatic moments and contestants competing for food and money. "It is often the constructedness of the setting of a reality TV show that foregrounds the authenticity of participants. If they appear to behave naturally in a contrived context, under surveillance, their authenticity is confirmed," argue Dubrofsky and Ryalls.[16] Performing not-performing is especially important on the set of *Big Brother* because CBS offers 24-hour surveillance of its houseguests.

This is not to say all *Big Brother* participants perform under the same cultural constrictions. Perceptions of authenticity are influenced by the social location, or identity, of the person deemed "authentic" or "inauthentic." Producers and viewers largely associate exaggerated displays of homosexuality as "authentically gay,"[17] much the same way "stereotypical representations of Black women on reality television come to represent supposed 'real' or 'authentic' Blackness."[18] Robin Boylorn encourages women of color to produce oppositional interpretations of Black women on reality TV programs. She argues that, "The oppositional reading understands the dominant interpretation but rejects it because it does not resonate with [the marginalized critic's] lived experience."[19] Like Boylorn, I use

32 "Just Be Yourself"

autoethnography to "both resist and relate to media representations, finding both commonality and contradictions" in how gay men are performatively rendered on reality television.[20]

Investigating performativity from an autoethnographic perspective underscores the phenomenological dynamics at play when an author internalizes and performs gendered and racialized expectations associated with his or her social location. The goal of phenomenological research, according to queer phenomenologist Jacqueline Martinez, is to explicate how time, place, and culture structure human consciousness.[21] Specifically, socio-historical context filters how we see the extra-mental world, or the physical space that exists outside of our minds. Martin Heidegger uses the term "intentionality" to describe how perception is always directed at something—real or imagined—and that directedness is what we use to make sense of lived experience. Heidegger reasons that "*Intentio* literally means *directing-itself-toward*. Every lived experience, every psychic comportment, directs itself toward something."[22] Perceptions position us in relation to the world and "pave the way in dealing with something."[23] Some/*thing* can be grounded in the material world or a figment of our imagination. Heidegger uses the example of strolling through the woods at night. He sees another man walking toward him. Is the other man dangerous? Should he run and hide? Intentionality characterizes the ways in which he orients himself in relation to the object, or man, in front of him. The shadowy figure turns out to be a tree. People often engage the psychic as real even when their individual perception does not reflect the physical world.

Intentionality sits at the core of our performative impulses. When *Big Brother* viewers see a gay contestant, intentionality directs their reading of him. A viewer might assume a gay man will cry more than his heterosexual counterparts or that a woman of color will have anger-management issues. Cultural scripts guide an audience's interpretation of a house guest; and any mundane action that verifies a stereotype affirms that the house guest is little more than the reductive images that have come to represent gays, lesbians, and people of color. Martinez continues:

> This "directedness" is what de Lauretis, citing Foucault and Peirce, refers to as a "technology of gender" but which can equally be understood as a "technology of race" or "technology of cultural difference." Thus race or cultural difference as we experience it is reproduced as a modality of experiencing that exists prior to the concrete "what" that we consciously know race or cultural difference to be—e.g., race as "real," cultural difference as knowable. Race or cultural difference is reproduced (embodied) at the level of modality, which is pre- or unconscious. It exists as a modality or way of going about perception and gives structure to our experience prior to our conscious awareness of experience.[24]

Intentionality governs our perceptions of other people's gender, sexuality, and race, and facilitates the psychic process by which we articulate and animate, or do, our own performance of identity.

Auditioning for a reality show allowed me to phenomenologically reflect on the *doing* of sexuality. My phenomenological impulses fired as I prepared for the final round of casting. I self-consciously exaggerated manners of speech and other behaviors that casting producers might read as gay. Intentionality guided my gay identity performance even before I met with Robyn Kass for the first time. A representative from Kassting, Inc. named Samantha called to work out the logistics of my hotel stay for finals. Samantha asked if I could arrive on Thursday, May 26, 2010. "Yikes," I said. "This is going to sound super gay but I have tickets to the midnight release of the *Sex and the City* sequel that night. Could I come on Friday?" Samantha squealed in delight. She was going to see the midnight showing, too. We spent five minutes rehashing our mutual adoration of the first *Sex and the City* film. During our conversation, I found myself playing the role of a straight woman's gay sidekick, like Stanford to Carrie on *Sex and the City*, Will and Jack to Grace and Karen on *Will & Grace*, and Marc St. James to Wilhelmina on *Ugly Betty*. I sometimes catch myself in self-conscious moments of queer performativity. The pitch of my voice increases. I say words like "girl" and "queen." These terms trigger me to recognize the performance *as I perform*. Robyn Kass, Samantha, and I know that, above and beyond anything else, I am auditioning to be Season 12's sole gay character. To win a spot on the show, I should play the part.

After I hung up with Samantha, I changed my outgoing message. "This is Ragan. Leave a message at the tone," was not gay enough. I wanted Robyn and Samantha to witness my proficiency in playing gay—even in the most mundane aspects of my life. I re-recorded my greeting to, "Hello, you've reached the phone of international supermodel Kelly Bensimon. Please. Leave. A. Message." Kelly Bensimon was one of the women featured on Bravo's reality program *The Real Housewives of New York*. Like many gays in West Hollywood, talking about *The Real Housewives* was my favorite pastime of 2010. My friend Mike and I performed quotations from *Housewives* like we were speaking a second language. I had no doubt Samantha, who worked on a reality show and lived down the street from FUBAR, my favorite West Hollywood haunt was fluent in *Housewives*. Even the name I selected sounded gay: Kelly Bensimon. Was Kelly named by drag queens?

One week later, I received a message from Samantha, who immediately expressed appreciation for my outgoing message. Samantha called to confirm my check-in time at the hotel. She also relayed a cautionary tale to emphasize how important it was for me to keep my lips locked about advancing to the final round of casting. The previous year a woman told her boyfriend that she made it to finals. He sent flowers to the hotel with a congratulatory note. Robyn saw the flowers in her room and immediately sent the woman home. Samantha explained that CBS has ways of finding out if I told anyone I was being considered for the show. She also instructed me to ignore guests at the hotel. Production does not want potential houseguests conversing until the game starts. If producers caught me talking to other people at the hotel, Robyn would send me home.

Like a good academic, I studied for casting's final exam. The Internet provides numerous anecdotes authored by people who have made it to the final round.

I listened to podcasts where Robyn Kass and *Big Brother*'s executive producer Allison Grodner discussed what they were looking for in a houseguest. Grodner explained that she loves casting people with unique professions. Fingers crashed against the keyboard as I searched the Web for and made a list of each past houseguest's job. *Big Brother* alumni include a former FBI agent, a video game expert, a neuroscientist, three firefighters, a bikini barista, and enough bartenders, waiters, and waitresses to staff a popular restaurant. The show has even featured a mortician. But no professors.

Casting as a Disciplinary Apparatus

Being there. May 28, 2010

I arrive to the hotel at 3 p.m. and am instructed to go to a fifteenth-floor suite after I have unpacked and settled. A handsome, dark-haired man named Jerry★ greets me when I get to the fifth floor. He hands me a time table for the rest of the day. The first event on the schedule is an IQ and personality assessment. Jerry informs me that the exam will take a few hours to complete, then I will break for dinner. Before he sends me to my hotel room, Jerry reminds me that I am not supposed to talk to anyone. Production has planted people in the hotel who will try to chat with me. If I mention anything about *Big Brother* they will send me home. If anyone approaches me, I should smile and politely end the conversation. I am not allowed to leave my room unless I have a scheduled appointment. I will eat with a group of other finalists at 7:45. Tomorrow's schedule includes an 11-o'clock breakfast, lunch in my room, pool time at 3:30, and gym time at 6. Jerry reveals that I could be here for an entire week or may be sent home tonight.

"I'll be here all week," I reply. Jerry chuckles and continues with the logistics of my stay. I am scheduled to meet with Dr. Jakobs★, the show psychologist tomorrow afternoon and with producers for a taped interview at 6 p.m. I should never say my name in common spaces of the hotel. He tells me to use my initials when checking into meals and recreation activities. Jerry encourages me to play against type when I am at dinner, in the gym, or at the pool. The goal is to make other potential contestants wonder who I am. Jerry ends our conversation with a casting tale from the previous year. A guy dressed up in dark sunglasses and a big hat each time he left his hotel room. Nothing conspicuous about that get-up, I think. I imagine him sunbathing in his hat, glasses, and an ankle-length London Fog trench coat. "Nothing to see here, folks," he stutters. Contrived example aside, Jerry's point is that the game has already started. Other finalists will be sizing me up and collecting information. I should do the same with them.

Jerry's recommendation is my first indication that I will be under constant surveillance. Surveillance performs two primary functions on a reality program

You will be called and invited to these appointmnets

SHOW APPOINTMENTS	ROOM NO.	Thursday 5/27	Friday 5/28	Saturday 5/29	Sunday 5/30	Monday 6/1	Tuesday 6/2	Wednesday 6/3	Thursday 6/4	Friday 6/5
PRODUCERS				6PM						
MEDICAL										
PSYCH A				1:30PM						
PSYCH B										
CALL BACK										
WRITTEN TEST			6PM							

ACTIVITIES

You will not be called to your activities but are expected to show up and check in

PERSONAL BREAKS	ROOM NO.	Thursday 5/25	Friday 5/26	Saturday 5/27	Sunday 5/28	Monday 5/29	Tuesday 5/30	Wednesday 5/31	Thursday 6/1	Friday 6/5
BREAKFAST	Café	11A —11:45	same	same	same	same	same	same	same	same
LUNCH	In your room	Rm Service	Rm Service	Rm Service	Rm Service	Rm Service	Rm Service	Rm Service	Rm Service	Rm Service
DINNER	Bar / Dining	7:45-8:30	same	same	same	same	same	same	same	same
POOL	Main floor	3:30-4:15	same	same	same	same	same	same	same	same
GYM	Main flloor	6p—7p	same	same	same	same	same	same	same	same

VERY IMPORTANT:

On travel days, you are not permitted to attend any of your activities. You must spend this day in your room, ordering room service, unpacking and relaxing.

FIGURE 2.2 My initial schedule for the final round of *Big Brother* auditions

36 "Just Be Yourself"

like *Big Brother*. First, Dubrofsky and Ryalls argue that surveillance confirms "consistency of character across disparate spaces: do participants appear to be the same people under surveillance they claim to be in their 'real' (unsurveilled) lives?"[25] Surveillance, in other words, confirms perceptions of authenticity.

Second, the fear of constant scrutiny helps production exercise disciplinary control over *Big Brother*'s onscreen talent. Producers groom potential houseguests to feel watched even when no cameras are in site. Weeks before I entered the hotel, Samantha convinced me that CBS had ways of knowing if I divulged to friends and family that I advanced to finals. A secret of this magnitude is torture for an exceedingly verbose man who lives his life in a constant state of TMI, or "too much information." Despite Samantha's warning, I told a handful of friends and family members that I made it to finals. The confessions threw me into a state of paranoia. Would CBS find out I blabbed? What were their "ways of knowing"? A panic attack knocked the wind out of my gut when I learned my friend Phil told a companion in New York that I might be on *Big Brother*'s next season. "This is how they find out," I thought. I tell a friend, and then that friend tells a few confidantes.

Big Brother is a contemporary, high-tech version of Jeremy Bentham's circular prison, the panopticon. In *Discipline and Punish*, Michel Foucault explores the metaphorical potential of Bentham's penitentiary, noting how its cylindrical architecture and central guard tower fool inmates into thinking guards might be watching them at any given moment. The threat of surveillance causes prisoners to police their own actions. Scholars have used panoptic gaze to theorize the ways in which school administrators monitor teachers,[26] mothers adjust their behavior in the presence of other mothers at neighborhood playgrounds,[27] companies record and review call center phone conversations to stifle employee resistance,[28] the Internet functions as a mode of social control,[29] and women self-monitor their bodies when reading fitness magazines.[30] Reality TV shows represent the ultimate extension of panoptic gaze, because an audience of millions is guaranteed to view a participant's behavior. Gaze is no longer a mere possibility in *Big Brother*'s panopticon; surveillance is a certainty.

Casting producers use panoptic techniques to manufacture easy-to-manipulate *Big Brother* houseguests. Foucault outlines four disciplinary mechanisms that produce docile bodies in panoptic structures: enclosures, partitions, exams, and time-tables (or strict schedules). Kass and her workers rigorously employ all four strategies in the final round of casting. First, finalists are sequestered at a hotel for an entire week. The hotel functions as an enclosure, or "protected place of disciplinary monotony."[31] The production team's use of *enclosures* is not unique to the final round of auditions. Before attending finals, I read that men and women ultimately cast on the show are also sequestered for nearly two weeks before they move into the house.

The pre-move-in sequester *partitions*, or isolates, houseguests to their hotel room. Partitioning teaches men and women in an enclosure that each person has his or her place, where place represents both physical space and social rank. There are obvious parallels between *Big Brother*'s sequester periods and the sort of solitary confinement found in a prison. Unlike the final round of auditions, contestants do not visit the pool, weight room, or hotel restaurants. Cast members are never allowed to leave their room. Production assistants bring contestants all their meals. The incoming group of competitors do not get to watch live television or make phone calls. At first glance, the sequester seems like a reasonable way to prepare the cast for their impending isolation in the *Big Brother* house. But isolated confinement also manufactures malleable, easy-to-control participants. Psychiatric studies overwhelmingly demonstrate that people who have undergone solitary confinement are more suggestible and easily persuaded than people who have not endured the rigors of forced and prolonged seclusion.[32] Can I make it through such a long period of isolation? The idea of spending two weeks in a hotel room causes goose pimples on my arm to stand at attention.

Next, the production team administers multiple exams to finalists. The assessments include an IQ test, a personality profile, a physical, a screening for sexually transmitted diseases, a drug test, and interviews with psychologists. For Foucault, examinations function as a "procedure of objectification and subjection."[33] The exams allow producers to collect behavioral, psychological, and intellectual information about each houseguest. Production can then use this data to incite desired effects from the cast. Media studies scholar Mark Andrejevich contends that "producers are not above tweaking the cast members' environment in order to generate interesting results."[34]

Finally, *time-tables* discipline insofar as they "establish rhythms, impose particular occupations, and regulate cycles of repetition."[35] Kass and her assistants dictate the times I eat, swim, exercise, take exams, am interviewed, and meet with doctors. Over an extended period, strict schedules governing when a finalist may leave his or her hotel room help produce compliant *Big Brother* houseguests.

Panopticons—whether they take the form of prisons or reality TV shows—train participants to become cogs in whichever disciplinary machine watches and governs over them. *Big Brother*'s intricate casting procedures are partially defined by an emergent irony, wherein Robyn Kass looks for unique, one-of-a-kind men and women, then subjects them to a series of disciplinary rituals that naturalizes conformity. "The individual body," Foucault argues, "becomes an element that may be placed, moved, articulated on others. Its bravery or its strength are no longer the principal variables that define it; but the place it occupies, the interval it covers, the regularity, the good order according to which it operates its movements."[36]

I marvel at how Jerry's and Samantha's suggestions of panoptic gaze, or fear of perpetual surveillance, have gotten into my head. They have recited the same monologues to hundreds—potentially thousands—of *Big Brother* hopefuls. Robyn Kass's procedures enable her to audition hundreds of finalists over the course of a week, collect information (e.g., IQ tests, psychological interviews, and personality

38 *"Just Be Yourself"*

profiles) about each potential houseguest, and indoctrinate a cast composed of bold personalities into obedient contestants. In sum, casting is not merely a process that determines who becomes a *Big Brother* houseguest. Casting inculcates. Kass's methods produce docile laborers.

A nuanced understanding of casting methods helps debunk a myth about reality television that is often perpetuated by the genre's producers, namely that "the control of specialists over the program has given way to that of the 'real' people it documents—non-specialists, just like the audience."[37] Reality programming creates the illusion of a democratic landscape. Cast members are not professional actors. They are everyday people selected from the ranks of average TV viewers. Jon Murray, co-producer of *The Real World* and *Road Rules*, has even suggested that "the roles of producer and audience have been reversed." Yet, Murray conveniently fails to mention the invisible control producers have over their cast and production. "Disciplinary power," writes Foucault, "is exercised through its invisibility. It is the subjects who have to be seen. Their visibility assures the hold of power that is exercised over them. It is the fact of being constantly seen, of being able always to be seen, that maintains the disciplined individual in his subjection."[38]

The uncomfortable pressure of surveillance is not foreign to me. I spent most of my childhood scrutinized by my peers. Schoolmates fixated on my presumed sexuality. Several years before my first same-sex kiss, boys and girls in my class tormented me each day with calls of "queer" and "faggot." I was not a kid who could pass for straight. Kids used my sexuality to justify their physical and emotional brutalization of me. Two decades later, my sexuality might oddly be the very thing that gets me on television. Still, the echo of past anti-gay prejudice leaves me feeling anxious.

The "written test" is my first appointment. I make my way to a conference room on the hotel's lobby level. A woman at the door snaps her fingers at me, indicating I need to check in at her desk. She asks for initials in a hushed tone.

"R. F."

Her right, poorly manicured index finger glides down a long page of initials. This is the first time I get a glimpse at how many people have been invited to finals. I estimate that 30 sets of initials are on the list. The top of her sheet reads "6 PM Group." Holy shit. How many groups are they testing? Hundreds of people could have made it this far into the audition process. The realization knocks me off my proverbial high horse. The conference room fills up with potential cast members. Two people sit at each of the room's 15 tables. A man in bifocals at the front of the room passes out exam packets and pencils and then provides instructions.

The first hour of the written test measures our IQ. Some questions focus on analytical reasoning, others are math-oriented. I take my time solving each puzzle and equation. I am only midway through the quiz when the tall guy in glasses abruptly announces our time is up. He collects our work, then hands each of us a Scantron and what appears to be a Myers-Briggs-style personality evaluation. The man explains that the test is not timed. After I bubble in my last answer, I should return to my room. The sheet asks hundreds of mind-numbing questions like, "Are you impressed by: a) principles, or b) emotions," and, "Motorcycles are: a) fun, or b) dangerous." None of the questions are difficult to answer but getting through 500 this-or-that queries would test the patience of even the most cool-headed person. A few preference selections make me audibly gasp and uncomfortably giggle. Do I hear voices? Have I ever hallucinated? Would I kill an animal for fun? The exam's authors sometimes ask the same question a variety of ways. Am I drawn to emotional or logical people? Are motorcycles risky or rewarding? Would I find it strange if a friend asked me to kill animals with him? It takes me an hour and a half to complete the questionnaire. When I return to the lobby for dinner, I notice some people from my testing group rolling their bags toward the hotel's entrance. Frowns and blank expressions indicate that they have already been sent home. That was fast.

The following day, I go to breakfast at 11:30. A production assistant located outside the first-floor restaurant asks for my initials. "R. F." I reply, wiping green crust from the corners of my eyes. Meagerly stabbing a fork in cold eggs and toast, I survey the room and take notes on other men and women in my breakfast group. One young, blonde woman is tanorexic, meaning her tan borders on chestnut stage makeup. White skin circles her eyes, leaving a pale imprint from the goggles she used in a tanning booth. "Reverse Panda," I scribble in my notepad. That is what she resembles: a film negative of a panda. My favorite characters on *Big Brother* provide biting commentary of other houseguests. Players visit the Diary Room, where they describe their fellow houseguests and narrate the week's significant events. Taking notes on other finalists will give me a proverbial leg-up when I meet with casting producers later today. I will come to our meeting armed with witty observations about other men and women in my dining, gym, and pool groups.

A Peri-performative Consideration of Performing Self

I meet with Dr. Jakobs, *Big Brother*'s resident psychologist at 1:30. Dr. Jakobs is a short White woman in her late 50s. She waves her pale, veiny hand toward a lumpy, maroon chair in her hotel room, indicating I should have a seat. Dr. Jakobs thumbs through various sheets of paper until she comes to what I presume to be my exam results from the previous night. Our conversation has a pleasant start. She asks me why I want to be on *Big Brother* and encourages me to talk about my familial relationships. The discussion takes an odd turn when her eyes fall to the paper in her hands and she declares that I am a risk taker.

"Not really," I say.

Dr. Jakobs insists that I am, nodding her head to my test results. My brows furrow and lips purse, as if an invisible rubber band were pulling the upper and lower parts of my face to my nose. "I'm actually not. I remember one of the questions asked about riding a motorcycle. I won't even sit on a parked motorcycle. I never have unsafe sex. I am one of the most predictable people on the planet. I order the same thing at each of my favorite restaurants. I won't even take a risk on trying a new salad." She maintains that I am incorrect. The exchange is odd and reminds me of the primary paradigmatic division between quantitative (i.e., objective) data and qualitative (i.e., subjective) research in my field, Communication Studies. Dr. Jakobs clings to a document that aims to break my character into easy-to-understand numbers. A Myers-Briggs Type Indicator is a peri-performative instrument therapists use to place respondents into basic personality types. I am a risk taker because the exam's algorithm points in that direction. The personality assessment exemplifies peri-performativity because the test "provides the textual conditions under which lives are narrated."[39] Dr. Jakobs oddly eschews important qualitative testimony that challenges the validity of her quiz. What motive do I have to lie about taking risks? If anything, risk-taking behavior might make me a sexier choice for casting producers. I leave my appointment with Dr. Jakobs in a bad mood. She has such limited knowledge of my personality and habits. Who is Dr. Jakobs to tell me who or what I am?

I return to my room and crack open a copy of George Chauncey's book *Gay New York*. Chauncey provides a historical account of gay men in New York at the turn of the century. Oddly enough, I am at a point in the text where he discusses the role nineteenth-century psychologists played in medicalizing homosexuality. For gay men, the doctor-patient relationship has historically characterized a hierarchical "structure that pits knower against known, that comes to exemplify the unequal relations through which scientific expertise asserts itself."[40] Regardless of Dr. Jakobs's intention, she placed me in a grid of intelligibility that connects homosexuality and risk-taking behavior. Questioning her findings made our meeting tense and unpleasant. Who was I to challenge her assessment of my predispositions? We had, after all, spent a total of 30 minutes in a hotel room together.

Conversation flows more organically when I meet with Robyn Kass and five other casting producers that evening. Two cameras are positioned to capture my profile and the front of my face. Three large, bright lights illuminate my seating area. Jerry instructs me to have a seat. This is the first time I have been face-to-face with Robyn Kass. Before coming to finals, I watched several YouTube videos in which she provided audition advice for reality TV hopefuls. Her petite figure, clear, olive complexion and caramel hair would make her an ideal candidate for *Big Brother*. She is only one year older than me but has been casting the show since its second season. Robyn takes out an enormous, white binder adorned with hundreds of Post-it placeholders and flips through several pages before she comes to my application.

Robyn quickly introduces me to her five associates. Jerry informs the group that I am a professor. "I primarily teach courses in rhetorical theory," I explain. Jerry arches an eyebrow, signaling he has no idea what rhetorical theory means.

"Just Be Yourself" **41**

"Rhetoric is just a fancy, schmancy term for persuasion," I tell the group. A thin, White guy with shaggy hair asks how my specialization in rhetoric will help me win *Big Brother*? Yes! This is a question I anticipated and an answer I rehearsed. "Persuasion is the most important skill in *Big Brother*, right? You've got to convince people to keep you in the house, then sway them to get rid of your enemies. One of the classes I teach is rhetorical theory. We cover 2000 years of Western thought, dating back to ancient Greece. I have two millennia of persuasive thought stored in my big, beautiful brain."

With a tilted head and inquisitive eyes, Robyn requests an example of a rhetorical theory I might use to win the game. "Dialectic, or the Socratic method, is one of the first theories I teach my undergraduate students. Socrates rarely came out and directly told a person what to think. Instead, he would ask about their opinions and then pose a series of questions to poke holes in their logic. By the end of the conversation, Socrates convinced his opponents that *his* ideas were *theirs*." This, of course, is a total bastardization of the Socratic method but the panel's wide eyes and furious notetaking indicate they have no idea that I have manipulated history to manipulate them. "I'll use dialectic in the house to get people to do what I want. The best part is that I'll never have to come out and directly say, 'Get rid of this person,' because the Socratic method is all about making the other person come to that conclusion. By never explicitly mentioning my targets I won't get blood on my hands."

Half of the men and women interviewing me sit with their mouths agape. The other three feverishly take notes as they bob their heads up and down in approval. A nerdy but cute guy looks up from a binder and introduces himself as Rich, one of the show's executive producers. He wants to know more about how I might use my profession to win the game. He is still trying to get a grasp of what it means to "study communication."

"Well," I respond, "one or two groups tend to dominate each season. And people love to name their alliances." At this point, I am off script. My heart quickens and palms sweat. Please, Ragan, do not ramble and stammer. Just talk to them like you are having a conversation with a friend. Be yourself. I fear I have rehearsed my presentation of self so diligently that I do not know how to simply be myself. "A communication expert will pay attention to those names because labels reveal something about the people who use them. Alliance names expose what a person celebrates and what they fear. That knowledge can be a person's undoing in a game like *Big Brother*."

Rich proposes that I work with a specific example. He fires off the name of the Renegades, a past *Big Brother* partnership that made it to the end of the game. Rich asks what their moniker reveals. "The two guys in the Renegades were alpha-male types: Dan and Memphis. The renegade title exudes masculinity. Guys like this lose their cool when you question their manliness. They become especially flustered if another man flirts with them. Those are the strings you have to pull to make that alliance fall apart."

42 "Just Be Yourself"

With a high-pitched excitement in her voice, Robyn requests that I deconstruct the name of more past *Big Brother* alliances. Almost everyone in the room laughs at her enthusiastic request. I feel like a magician at a kid's birthday party. Jerry and I share a smile. I told you I'd be here all week, Jerry. After I talk about a few more *Big Brother* alliances, the team asks me what I think about the other finalists. "I've developed names for the people in my dining group," I confess. I tell them about Reverse Panda, Pudgy Pirate, and other poor souls for whom I have developed unflattering nicknames. My gestures become more pronounced and expressive, and the tone of my voice climbs an octave as I share my observations. The more the panel laughs, the more I amp up my queer performance.

After an exhilarating interview, I return to my hotel room and turn on the television. NBC's talent competition *America's Got Talent* blares on the TV. Awful. I walk to the nightstand and grab *Gay New York*. Suddenly, the sound of a brittle knuckle rapping against a door breaks my focus. I make my way to the room's entrance. A producer is at my neighbor's door. My right ear hovers against the doorframe, straining to hear the conversation.

"I'm sorry," a sad-sounding woman states. "I fought for you. I did. This just isn't your year. They loved you and think you'd be great but not this season."

"Did I press the villain angle too much," my hotel neighbor inquires.

"No, not at all. They loved the entire bitch thing you had going on."

The percussion-beat of my heart reverberates through my body. Listening to this conversation seems wrong. I step away from the door. What if I'm next? What if the producer finishes up with the would-be villain and then there's a knock on my door? Please don't knock. Casting raven, don't come rapping on my chamber door.

Turning People Into Characters

Being here

Throughout various audition interviews, casting producers encouraged me to, "Just be myself." Their questions and coaching clued me into the sort of "self" that would most likely win one of 13 coveted spots on *Big Brother*'s twelfth season. Robyn Kass works with several casting associates, each of whom is responsible for a pool of potential contestants. Samantha served as my liaison to Robyn and the show's producers. She proposed various roles I might play on Season 12. Had I been sent home early, Samantha's knuckle would have been the one knocking on my hotel room door. Kass's associates become personally invested in the applicants they represent. One of their finalists being cast on the show is a testament to their advocacy and a mark of professional achievement. In a podcast interview with *Big Brother* 8 winner Dan Gheesling,

"Just Be Yourself" **43**

Kass explicates the process her team uses to pitch characters to the show's executive producers. She says:

> We are not going to sit and watch 30 minutes on each of these people. We jump to like a 30-second spot where they are funny, or energetic or something cool. [My team] might comment to me and say, "Okay so I have this sound bite from them, watch this." We decide how we want to paint their picture. We do write ups, like pitch sheets on everybody. We have their picture. You talk about the type of person they are and a little bit of their background.[41]

The narratives Kass's team craft for finalists often lay a season's narrative groundwork. Take, for example, the mafia-oriented story producers used to performatively engender Enzo, Season 12's sole Italian American contestant. In the house, Enzo revealed that his casting interviews largely centered around him adopting a crime-boss persona in the game. He told Kass' team that he would have a team of hit men who would do all his dirty work. He planned to call his group Enzo's Angels. The Angels would include a girl with big boobs, a gay guy, and a muscle head. Enzo referenced many character archetypes audiences have come to expect in *Big Brother*. Through their questions and prodding, casting producers encouraged Enzo to build upon the mafia narrative.

While filming, I did not realize how Enzo's tale, which started in preliminary casting interviews, shaped our season's anchoring story. Enzo was one member of a four-man alliance called the Brigade. He was not responsible for creating the coalition but story editors used diary room question-answer periods to create the illusion that Enzo was the "boss" of the Brigade. Enzo, after all, had rehearsed the mafia narrative over the course of multiple casting interviews. In the second episode, Enzo explains in a confessional segment that, "When you start a mafia, you have to go to the guy who's in charge. This week, that's Hayden. The next thing you got to do is have some brains in this operation." The camera cuts to Enzo talking to Matt, the season's self-proclaimed "evil genius." Enzo continues, "And every mafia needs some type of a muscle, which I call Lane. He's the size of a tree, this guy."

Story producers eventually cast aside Enzo's mafia metaphor after his alliance named itself the Brigade, a term that reflects military strategy, not organized crime. Enzo's mafia narrative highlights the ways in which casting influences a season's narrative before cameras have even started to roll. Derek Kompare writes that:

> While the people and events in these programs need to be demonstrably "real"—not acting—to satisfy generic requirements, they are cast and planned as carefully as in any fiction. Both the casting and the limited scope of events allow for what might be called "maximum control of conditions of spontaneity": narrowing the likely range of actions to those with the greatest visual or narrative impact.[42]

44 "Just Be Yourself"

By repeatedly casting stock characters, Kass and executive producer Allison Grodner have mastered the art of controlling the sort of "spontaneous" conflicts that surface in the house year after year.

Character archetypes represent *Big Brother*'s principal peri-performative constraints. Almost every season includes a gay man, a Black man or woman, an athlete, an airhead, and a middle-aged person. Although the names of the characters change from one season to the next, viewers can expect a scene where a gay contestant teaches a heterosexual houseguest about homophobia's nuances, or the sports star reveals that he is more than just a "meat head." Repeatedly casting the same types of characters allows producers to shape the interactions viewers witness.

Kass and Grodner's peri-performative strategies are painstakingly premeditated even when they cast outside the typical *Big Brother* archetypes. *Big Brother*'s production team is plugged into the United States zeitgeist and often follows trends started by other popular reality TV programs. It is no coincidence that Enzo was cast on *Big Brother* a mere six months after MTV's Italian American-oriented reality show *Jersey Shore* became a headline-catching, ratings hit. Four years later, CBS cast a 44-year-old, White school groundskeeper from North Carolina named Donny Thompson. Donny's backwoods persona is amplified by a long, salt-and-pepper beard, camouflage wardrobe, and southern twang. Donny replicated a character type popularized the previous year on A&E's hit reality TV show *Duck Dynasty*. One year later and on the heels of Olympic champion Kaitlyn Jenner coming out as transgender, *Big Brother 17* included its first transgender houseguest.

Casting producers also use backstage interactions with finalists to establish peri-performative control over the future cast. During the final round of auditions, Samantha periodically visited me during meals at the hotel and offered self-presentation tips, like the right clothes to wear and personal information to emphasize. Her advice proved helpful the two additional times I met with producers at the hotel.

Seven days feels like an eternity when you are stuck in a hotel room. I never knew when producers would call me in for another filmed interview. I spent hours playing on my iPad, rehearsing personal narratives, trying to formulate catchphrases, watching soap operas, and daydreaming about how my life might change if I made it on *Big Brother*. A production assistant finally notified me on day six that I would be heading to CBS studios the following day. He revealed that the CBS trip is the furthest anyone can go in the casting process.

Being there. June 4, 2010

I tossed and turned last night. Adrenaline coursed through my body and questions flooded my brain. How many finalists made it this far? Am I the only gay guy meeting with CBS executives? What kind of questions will they ask? A 20-something casting assistant escorts me from my hotel room to one of three 18-passenger vans.

"Just Be Yourself"   **45**

The P.A. commands me to ignore everyone in the van and avoid eye contact. Talking to other finalists is forbidden. Fourteen other men join me in the vehicle. All but one of us are White. I jam Apple headphones into my ears and stare out the window. Lady GaGa's disco-like music puts me in a trance.

> *I'm your biggest fan*
> *I'll follow you until you love me*
> *Papa-Paparazzi*
> *Baby there's no other superstar*
> *You know that I'll be your*
> *Papa-Paparazzi*

Am I the only one who thought to bring an iPod? The driver makes his way down the 405 in mid-morning traffic. We arrive at CBS Studios 40 minutes later. The guy at the wheel informs us that the outside of the *Big Brother* house is directly to our right. Everyone immediately spins to the right and "oohs" and "aahs" over a structure that looks nothing like a house. All we can make out is a three-story fence that appears around the perimeter of what I assume to be the backyard. The cliché "so close yet so far away" has never felt truer to me than in this moment.

Two other white vans pull up next to us. Both automobiles are packed with women. Most of the guys look at the other vehicles like they are staring at piñatas filled with the most decadent, mouth-watering treats. A few even grunt their enthusiastic approval. What a bunch of cavemen. Robyn Kass exits her Range Rover and enters our van. She places her knees on the seat next to the driver and paints a picture of how the day will transpire. Robyn explains that we are going to spend six to eight hours sitting in a café on the lot. We are not allowed to speak to any of the other finalists. Last night, Robin's team put together three to five–minute sizzle reels of each person in the van. The tapes showcase our best moments throughout the audition process. Robin gleefully discloses that we are about to meet the folks who have the final say on casting for all the big reality shows, like *The Amazing Race*, *Survivor*, and *Big Brother*. Nobody gets into the *Big Brother* house without first seeing the wizards behind CBS's reality TV curtain.

Sitting in a café on the CBS Studios lot, I silently eyeball 35 men and women. Each person in the sweet-smelling establishment has a doppelganger, or look-alike, who poses a threat. My doppelganger is a young, thin Latino. His bright purple scarf, tight-fitting pants, legs crossed at the knees, and expressive hand gestures lead me to believe that he is gay. I have seen enough reality shows to know that television executives rarely cast two gay men—let alone two effeminate gay men—in a single season. True to mythological form, my doppelganger portends jeopardy in this final round of casting. He is the only other person from my meal group who made it to the CBS interview. I called him Sideshow Bob in my notes. Sideshow Bob is a recurring character on *The Simpsons*. Both Bobs sport a palm

46 "Just Be Yourself"

tree-like hairstyle that is long, curly, and spiked in every possible direction. Who will producers cast: my sexual mirror image or me?

The final interview gives me an idea of how Robyn pitched my character. Each of the ten TV executives stares in my direction. Robyn breaks the ice by asking where I am from. "A town called Cypress, Texas, which is on the outskirts of Houston. Cypress was a terrible place to be a gay teenager. There was a jukebox in my high school cafeteria that only played country music. Some kids from the neighborhood shot a donkey—probably because they had sex with it. Growing up in a place like that can be isolating but it made me dig deep for resources." The group smiles. The next questions focus on my profession. When did I know that I wanted to be a teacher?

"When I was I kid," I explain. "I lured friends over to my place with the promise of toys. The only condition is that we had to play school, and I was the teacher. My father used to get angry because I'd draw on the garage walls like they were a blackboard. One year for Christmas I even asked my dad if he'd get me an overhead projector. I was probably the only kid in my class who thought an overhead projector would be the all-time best present." The group chuckles at my confession.

A stocky, frizzy-haired, middle-aged White woman asks what I wear when I teach.

"Just jeans and a t-shirt," I tell her.

Her lips bow to a half-frown. The executive says she imagines a professor in a bowtie, like the professor from *Gilligan's Island*. I get the feeling her statement is a gentle request, as if to say, "We want our *Big Brother* professor in a bowtie."

Robyn asks me to share my thoughts on the other finalists who made it to the CBS lot. Like an up-and-coming standup comic, I repeat a few "best hits" from earlier audition rounds. I also work in some new material collected during the two mind-numbing hours I spent seated in silence at the CBS café. "And who is the guy with red hair and Oakley sunglasses? Red hair *and* Oakley sunglasses. That's just adding insult to injury," I joke. "Last night, I saw him eating dinner and he had his sunglasses on the back of his head. Is that fashion?" The group laughs.

The woman with frizzy hair points out to her colleagues that I pay attention to people.

"I collect information," I explain. "I'm prepared to knock somebody down a peg when necessary. I was bullied as a kid. I put up with a lot of bullshit. Kids in my class spit at me and called me 'faggot,' and I just sat in silence and took it. The abuse happened every day. Around my sophomore year of high school, I said, 'If this is going to end, if people are going to stop messing with me, I have to hit back.' I sat back and observed people. I was trying to find their insecurities. Once I figure out your weakness, I'll exploit it. This is a survival skill I took with me into adulthood." Wow. Given how much I rehearsed my answers, I am surprised such an earnest and spontaneous confession fell from my lips. *Big Brother* auditions have, in several moments, felt like a talking cure, or speech-oriented form of therapy. After 15 minutes of conversation, I return to the café.

Two weeks pass before a woman named Sheila★ calls to inform me that CBS wants to send a cameraman to my school to get some footage of me teaching. The moment Sheila mentions a camera operator coming with me to class, I know I have been cast. Every season of *Big Brother* starts the same way. The first 15 minutes of each premiere features footage of the houseguests at work or involved in some sort of hobby. A friend, coworker, or loved one then surprises the finalist with an oversized key to the *Big Brother* house. The key has the contestant's name etched into it and will eventually be used to represent the houseguest's safety in nomination ceremonies. Sheila emphasizes that no casting decisions have been made. I play along with Sheila. "I totally understand," I say in a hushed tone, trying my best to contain my excitement.

The next week is chaotic. CBS does not want me to tell anyone that I am being considered for the program. But Sheila warns me that I need to prepare to leave at a moment's notice. CBS's mixed messages make it difficult to navigate my university's bureaucracy. I am in the middle of teaching a summer class and may have to miss three weeks of the fall semester, depending on how far I get in the game.

My heart sinks when officials at Cal State, Long Beach inform me that CBS does not have permission to visit campus and film. Sheila and her team suggest that we rent a space in West Hollywood. She encourages me to invite students and a few friends. The field producer will make whatever place CBS rents look like a classroom. The important thing is that they get footage of me teaching. Sheila urges me to look the part, or dress like a professor.

One week later, I arrive at West Hollywood's Gay and Lesbian Center dressed in dark jeans, a blue button-up shirt, and a bowtie. Factoring in my high school prom and a friend's wedding, this is only the third time in my life I have worn a bowtie. If CBS wants a professor in a bowtie, that is precisely what I will give them. I greet a group of seven students, who receive extra credit for attending. They mention how professional I look. My students have never seen me so formally dressed. We enter a corner room, where I deliver a lecture on Michel Foucault and the panopticon. My Foucault presentations tend to be among my students' favorites. Best of all, panoptic themes are consistent with the kind of surveillance one would encounter in the *Big Brother* house. A student named Dorit★ raises her hand midway through the lecture. When I call on her, she "surprises" me with my key to the house. I do my best to act genuinely shocked by the news. "Get out of here," I exclaim. Everyone in the room claps and hoots.

Greg★, the field producer, asks if we can film the key reveal again. He wants a more dramatic response from the group. I burst out laughing at Greg's request. The more I try to compose myself, the more I grow unhinged. "I just need a moment," I plead. Lisa Kudrow's character Valerie Cherish keeps popping into my brain. Valerie is the main character of my favorite HBO sitcom, *The Comeback*. In its pilot episode, a reality TV camera crew follows the has-been sitcom star as she auditions for a part in a network comedy. Valerie's reality TV production team sits her down after she learns she won a spot on the show.

48 "Just Be Yourself"

"Well, I got it," she cheerfully discloses in a confessional segment. A producer named Jane cuts Valerie off before she can share more thoughts. The producer asks her to do it again. "Sure," she agrees. "Was there a technical problem?"

"I think you can be a little bigger, a little more excited," Jane encourages.

"Ok. Can do," Valerie smiles. She turns her attention back to the camera. "Well, I got it," Valerie repeats with a bit more enthusiasm.

"I'm sorry," Jane once again interrupts. "It's just the whole comeback is about how excited you are. This needs to be the big event."

"Ok, I got you." Valerie takes a deep breath and turns back to the camera. "Well, I got it!"

"Can you do it again?"

"Jane, I'm sorry. I don't want to look like an idiot. This is supposed to be reality."

"I just think your reality can be more excited. Just one more. For safety."

Valerie's eyes shoot laser beams of aggression through Jane. She gets up from her chair, walks away from the camera for a few seconds, and then returns. "Well, I got it!" Valerie's enthusiasm instantly gives way to insecurity. "Ok, you can't use that. That's a crazy person."

Who am I in this moment? A professor teaching in a staged environment? A token gay guy about to join the cast of a reality show? Am I Valerie Cherish? Ragan playing Valerie playing a college professor? We repeat the key reveal a few times and feign surprise for the camera. Like Valerie toward the end of her "I got it" scene, our reactions become irritatingly animated. An older gentleman enters the room and asks us to "tone it down." "We're conducting a memorial service in the room right next to you," he explains. Greg apologizes on our behalf and tells the gentleman that we are wrapping up.

The cameraman and Greg confiscate my cellphone and then drive me back to my apartment, where two of my best friends wait for us. The camera films me as I pretend to pack clothes into a *Big Brother* duffle bag furnished by CBS. Sheila intimated that I should have a packed suitcase ready "just in case." Greg removes a stack of shirts from my luggage and tells me to slowly re-fold the tops and place some of them in the *Big Brother* bag. The cameraman futzes around with lighting in my bedroom so the scene will be well-lit. He eventually grabs some lamps from the living room and places them in the corners of my bedroom.

Blood rushes to my face. The magnitude of the moment weighs me down. Sweat drips from my hairline and down now-crimson cheeks. All the lights in the room make me feel like I am trapped in a microwave oven. Greg hands me a few tissues so that I can remove sweat from my face. Once the room is finally lit to the cameraman's satisfaction, we start filming again. This is the precise moment I begin filtering all my behaviors through a self-conscious reality TV filter. Will this bit make it to TV? How will the audience respond to what I am about to say?

Could this utterance get me fired from my job? Am I making good television? "Reality" has now split into two timelines: lived experience and edited TV footage intended to represent my life.

Lived experience/CBS's edited footage

RAGAN: Holy cow. How does a gay person pack in an hour?
  (Greg asks me a series of questions):
GREG: *What would you be willing to do to stay in the house?*
HAYDEN: I would be willing to flirt with a gay guy,
  if it meant staying in the house another week.
GREG: *What type of people do you want to find in the house?*
RAGAN: I have a thing for big, dumb guys.
  They got the brawn but I've got the brain.
  I can make them do what I want.
LANE: I would like to buddy up with somebody who's smart.
  That way I don't have to do the thinking.

What kind of personalities do I want to avoid seeing? What is my strategy for winning the game? These are all topics covered during my interviews so I repeat my answers—all of which have been well-rehearsed by this point. The filming session lasts roughly 15 minutes. Greg explains that I have five minutes to say bye to my dog and friends. I hug my pals who provide last-minute advice. "Don't trust anyone," my buddy Mike instructs. My friend Peter adds, "Don't come home without the money."

I reserve my final farewell for my yellow Labrador, Bella. This is the only moment that feels painfully slow. Bella's limbs shake with anxiety. Tears bubble around the cracks of my eyes. How will I make it months without Bella? Will she remember me when I return? I throw my arms around Bella's neck and tightly squeeze her.

Britney tearfully hugs goodbye to her father.
Matt kisses his wife.
Lane embraces his mother.
Enzo holds his baby daughter.
The gay guy bids farewell to his dog.

Greg ushers me outside and into his car. We make our way to a hotel as the cameraman films my friends waving goodbye in my driveway. Forty minutes later, we arrive at a hotel in Studio City. This will be my home for the next two weeks. No phone calls. No television. No leaving the room. I am about to be on national television.

50 "Just Be Yourself"

Notes

1 Sarah Banet-Weiser and Laura Portwood-Stacer, "'I Just Want to Be Me Again!' Beauty Pageants, Reality Television, and Post-feminism," *Feminist Theory* 7, no. 2 (2006): 265.

2 Spencer E. Cahill, William Distler, Cynthia Lachowetz, Andrea Meaney, Robyn Tarallo, and Teena Willard, "Meanwhile Backstage: Public Bathrooms and the Interaction Order," *Journal of Contemporary Ethnography* 14, no. 1 (1985): 33–58.

3 John O'Brien, "Spoiled Group Identities and Backstage Work: A Theory of Stigma Management Rehearsals," *Social Psychology Quarterly* 74, no. 3 (2011): 291–309.

4 Simon Lewin and Scott Reeves, "Enacting 'Team' and 'Teamwork': Using Goffman's Theory of Impression Management to Illuminate Interprofessional Practice on Hospital Wards," *Social Science and Medicine* 72, no. 10 (2011): 1595–1602.

5 Lisa Sarmicanic, "Goffman, Pets, and People: An Analysis of Humans and Their Companion Animals," *ReVision* 27, no. 2 (2004): 42–7.

6 Erving Goffman, *The Presentation of Self in Everyday Life* (Woodstock: Overlook, 1973), 123.

7 Ibid., 113.

8 Ibid., 128.

9 Eve Kosofsky Sedgwick, *Touching Feeling: Affect, Pedagogy, Performativity* (Durham, NC: Duke University Press, 2003).

10 Kurt Spellmeyer, "Foucault and the Freshman Writer: Considering the Self in Discourse," *College English* 51, no. 7 (1989): 715.

11 To help distinguish between reconstructed moments of the past depicted in the present tense ("being there") and instances of scholarly reflection ("being here"), I borrow Tami Spry's "being there"/"being here" sequencing from her essay "Performing Autoethnography." Spry's organization is an adaptation of Geertz's celebrated distinction of "being there" and "being here"; Tami Spry, "Performing Autoethnography: An Embodied Methodological Praxis," *Qualitative Inquiry* 7, no. 6 (2001): 706–32; Clifford Geertz, *Works and Lives: The Anthropologist as Author* (Stanford, CA: Stanford University Press, 1988).

12 Lyle Masaki, "Big Brother: Excusing Bad Behavior?" *Logo*, last modified August 13, 2007, accessed February 22, 2017, www.newnownext.com/big-brother-excusing-bad-behavior/08/2007/.

13 Andy Denhart, "The Best and the Worst of Reality TV in 2007," *Today*, last modified December 26, 2007, accessed February 22, 2017, www.today.com/popculture/best-worst-reality-tv-2007-wbna22364117.

14 Names accompanied by an asterisk are pseudonyms. I use real names when a person's identity is made obvious by the situation. Most hardcore fans, for instance, know that Robyn Kass is *Big Brother*'s head casting producer and Allison Grodner is the show's executive producer.

15 Rachel E. Dubrofsky and Emily D. Ryalls, "The Hunger Games: Performing No-Performing to Authenticate Femininity and Whiteness," *Critical Studies in Media Communication* 31, no. 5 (2014): 396.

16 Rachel E. Dubrofsky and Emily D. Ryalls, "The Hunger Games," 398.

17 Michaela Meyer and Jennifer Kelley, "Queering the Eye? The Politics of Gay White Men and Gender (In)visibility," *Feminist Media Studies* 4 (2004): 214–17.

18 Robin Boylorn, "As Seen on TV: An Autoethnographic Reflection on Race and Reality Television," *Critical Studies in Media Communication* 25, no. 4 (2008): 421.

19 Ibid., 414.

20 Ibid.

21 Jacqueline M. Martinez, "Semiotic Phenomenology and Intercultural Communication Scholarship: Meeting the Challenge of Racial, Ethnic, and Cultural Difference," *Western Journal of Communication* 70, no. 4 (2006): 297.

"Just Be Yourself"   **51**

22 Martin Heidegger, *History of the Concept of Time: Prolegomena*, trans. Theodore Kisiel (Bloomington: Indiana University Press, 1992), 29.
23 Ibid.
24 Jacqueline M. Martinez, "Semiotic Phenomenology and Intercultural Communication Scholarship," 297.
25 Rachel E. Dubrofsky and Emily D. Ryalls, "The Hunger Games," 398.
26 Mary Bushnell, "Teachers in the Schoolhouse Panopticon: Complicity and Resistance," *Education and Urban Society* 35, no. 3 (2003): 251–72.
27 Holly Blackford, "Playground Panopticism: Ring-Around-the Children, A Pocketful of Women," *Childhood* 11, no. 2 (2004): 227–49.
28 Peter Bain and Phil Taylor, "Entrapped by the 'Electronic Panopticon'?" *Worker Resistance in the Call Centre, New Technology, Work and Employment* 15, no. 1 (2000): 2–18.
29 Russell Spears and Martin Lea, "Panacea or Panopticon? The Hidden Power in Computer-Mediated Communication," *Communication Research* 21, no. 4 (1994): 427–59.
30 Margaret Carlisle Duncan, "The Politics of Women's Body Images and Practices: Foucault, The Panopticon and Shape Magazine," *Journal of Sport and Social Issues* 18, no. 1 (1994): 48–65.
31 Michel Foucault, *Discipline and Punish: The Birth of the Prison*, trans. Alan Sheridan (New York, NY: Vintage Books, 1977), 141.
32 Richard H. Walters, John E. Callagan, and Albert F. Newman, "Effect of Solitary Confinement on Prisoners," *The American Journal of Pscyhiatry* 119, no. 8 (1963): 771.
33 Michel Foucault, *Discipline and Punish*, 192.
34 Mark Andrejevic, "The Kinder, Gentler Gaze of Big Brother: Reality TV in the Era of Digital Capitalism," *New Media & Society* 4, no. 2 (2002): 261.
35 Michel Foucault, *Discipline and Punish*, 149.
36 Ibid., 164.
37 Mark Andrejevic, "The Kinder, Gentler Gaze of Big Brother," 260.
38 Ibid., 187.
39 Anna Poletti, "Periperformative Life Narrative: Queer Collages," *GLQ: A Journal of Gay and Lesbian Studies* 22, no. 3 (2016): 359.
40 Lynne Huffer, *Mad for Foucault: Rethinking the Foundations of Queer Theory* (New York, NY: Columbia University Press, 2009), 142.
41 Robyn Kass, interview by Dan Gheesling, *How to Get on Reality TV*, podcast audio, April 3, 2013, http://traffic.libsyn.com/howtogetonrealitytv/HGR010.mp3.
42 Derek Kompare, "Extraordinarily Ordinary: The Osbournes as 'An American Family'," *Reality TV: Remaking Television Culture*, ed. Susan Murray and Laurie Ouellette (New York, NY: New York University Press, 2009), 109.

3

"FAGAN: AWESOME REPRESENTATIVE OF THE GAY COMMUNITY"

Being there. June 28, 2010

TV Guide's Michael Logan and I sit in a drab hotel conference room. He takes out a beat-up Dictaphone, presses record, and asks what I do for a living, "I am a professor of communication at California State University, Long Beach," I tell him.

Mr. Logan questions why a college professor would agree to be on a show like *Big Brother*. He is the third consecutive reporter to pose this question. I smile and tell him, "I started this insane journey, in part, because of my job. In a bulk of my research, I look at how gay men perform their identities in different contexts, ranging from interpersonal interactions to theatrical stages. *Big Brother* is Shakespearian. The show takes place on a stage, albeit a soundstage; includes heroes and villains; features dramatic themes, like war, love, and loss; and may incite catharsis in its millions of viewers."

Narratization as an Interpretive Model

Being here

Competition-driven reality programs, like *Survivor* and *The Amazing Race*, are filmed months before they are edited and aired. Story producers on those shows know who ultimately won the competition before they begin editing the first episode, which gives them the benefit of retroactive sense making. *Big Brother* is unique because the program is broadcast as it is filmed. Producers on *Big Brother* are not privy to who will ultimately win the game; nor do they know how other forms of game-related power will shift from one week to the next. Constructing narratives on the set of *Big Brother* is hard work because story producers can only anticipate (rather than definitively know) how the competition might unfold. Because *Big Brother's* theatricality largely depends on how its contestants, story editors, and producers perceive potential outcomes of interactions and competitions, I turn to phenomenological understandings of narrative to explicate how the program's tales and characters are produced.

Phenomenological explanations of narrative are significantly different from the oft-celebrated structural interpretation of narration championed by rhetorician Walter Fisher. According to Fisher, people use narratives to make sense of the world. Narrative structure projects temporal relationships, heroes, and villains on chaotic phenomena. Much like a *Survivor* producer, we narrate retroactively or after we have experienced a series of disordered events.[1] Phenomenologists, on the other hand, claim that humans are "storylivers," or that temporal expectations of a story shape the way we perceive phenomena, regardless of whether or not we know the beginning of a tale or have witnessed its conclusion.[2] If, for instance, I hear a woman scream in the halls of my apartment building, my brain fills in the missing blanks of her tale. "Maybe she's being mugged," I think. "I bet the perpetrator is male." Regardless of why the woman screams in the hall, the narrative I create situates my consciousness in a particular reality and incites me to act in specific ways, like calling the police.

Narrative residue from the past and future narrative possibilities work in a concomitant, dialogic fashion to mold human perception while we are in the midst of making decisions. This phenomenological process is known as "narratization."[3] Edmund Husserl, the "father" of phenomenology, claims that memory or phenomenological "retention" shapes our understandings of the present and expectations of the future, insofar as what has been perpetually echoes what may, once again, come to be.[4] "Protention" characterizes our expectations, or how the various stories that comprise our lives may conclude.[5] A contestant on *Big Brother*, for example, may justify lying and backstabbing if he or she has seen those strategies work in previous seasons of the show (retention) and believes similar performances may increase his or her ability to win $500,000 (protention).

I reference theories of narratization to help explicate the lived aspects of *Big Brother*. Storyliving, in this book, characterizes a phenomenological process by which *Big Brother* producers, the show's fans, and I used retained information (i.e., the past) and anticipations of the future to narratize characters and storylines. Narratization functions like a perceptual toolbox, where everyone involved in the show finds instruments with which to build, edit, and tear down *Big Brother's* narrative and the players in it. Producers use editing to construct tales and characters, and, in the midst of participation, reality TV personalities edit themselves. Unfortunately, moment-to-moment acts of self-production are rarely explicated

54 Fagan: Awesome Representative

in scholarly terms. I am particularly interested in how producers, fans, and I referenced and co-produced feminized tropes of gay men.

Narratizing via Tropes of Gay Representation

Narratization presupposes absence, or character and narrative-related voids that retention and protention eventually fill. *Big Brother's* production team played a significant role in rhetorically constructing the "missing blanks" of my sexuality. Their gay-erasure techniques are not new, nor unique to reality television. Gay characters on TV are "rarely shown in their own communities, homes, or same-sex romantic relationships but are depicted in terms of their place in the lives of heterosexuals."[6] My symbolic isolation proved particularly salient on Thursdays, when producers regularly aired friends-and-family packages. In these five-minute segments, loved ones of houseguests describe each competitor outside the context of the game. The taped features help humanize *Big Brother* contestants and show their connections to broader communities. Out of the final seven houseguests, I was the only one who did not receive a friends-and-family segment.

Isolation of gay characters is also rhetorically depicted by way of symbolic impotence, or lack of same-sex intimacy. Network reality shows tend to cast only one gay male character a season, so it is rare to see sexual minorities involved in a romantic coupling (or "showmance"), or engage in any sex act that might be marked as gay. Early in the game, I felt left out when my roommates discussed potential romantic pairings among the houseguests. Gay characters on TV are "often marked by a failure to communicate and achieve intimacy."[7] Take, for example, Will from the NBC sitcom *Will & Grace*. Will is rendered symbolically impotent, because, unlike his heterosexual counterpart Grace, viewers never see him in bed with other men or engage in any significant form of gay intimacy. Shugart notes that most depictions of gay men in the popular media "skirt the realities and implications of homosexuality by almost never depicting [gay men] in romantic or sexual situations."[8] Likewise, gay men on mainstream reality shows like *Queer Eye for the Straight Guy* are only able to join the ranks of televisual representation "as long as they do not infer any sexual desires and practices."[9]

Because gay characters are typically denied opportunities for romantic involvement and may not perform their identities via sex acts, producers, fans, and LGBTQ characters must find other ways to performatively render non-normative sexual identity, or, in phenomenological terms, "fill in the missing blanks" of gay sexuality. As media critic Alexander Doty explains, "Queerness is frequently expressed in ways other than by nude bodies in contact, kissing, or direct verbal indicators."[10] Queer sexuality is commonly engendered by way of stereotypical, repetitious representations of gay people that media construct and propagate.[11] Televised enactments of gay identity take the form of several tropes of representation, including the crying gay man; the villain motif;[12] the trope of excessive gay femininity;[13] the figure of "gay pretenders," or heterosexual people who perform a gay façade;[14] the image of gay-by-association heterosexual characters, who are mistakenly marked as homosexual because they interact with queer people;[15] and the trope of "gay-man/hetero-gal duos" that bolster heteronormativity by mimicking heterosexual couplings.[16]

Borrowing terminology from Gerbner and Gross,[17] Fejes and Petrich liken negative and limited portrayals of homosexuals in the media to a "symbolic annihilation" of gays and lesbians.[18] Paradoxical interplay between symbolic construction and "annihilation" pulls gay characters into a perhaps inescapable web of representation, where their communicative moves are read, anticipated, and reworked to fit into pre-existing roles that "not only define them, but define as well an oxymoronic gay sexuality which is puritanical, self-regulating, and willing to sacrifice itself in the protection of heterosexual integrity."[19]

Producing Self via Autoethnography

Communication scholars have utilized qualitative research methods to map webs of stereotype-driven representation and conduct oppositional readings of reality TV shows. But these critical and sometimes autoethnographic accounts are typically told from the viewers' perspective. Robin Boylorn, for instance, details her response to representations of Black women on reality TV shows and, using autoethnography, tries to reconcile the sometimes complementary, sometimes contradictory, roles of reality television fan and media critic.[20] Like Boylorn, I turn to autoethnography to explore multiple characters that I performed in 2010, including performance scholar, educator, and the only gay male character in the twelfth season of *Big Brother*. Positioned inside TVs representational machine, I critically investigate how, in the absence of gay sex acts, producers and I performatively enacted gay identity in the *Big Brother* house. In other words, how did we sometimes consciously and sometimes unwittingly use tropes of gay identity performance to narratize my character?

Tropes of gay representation are residual, retention-oriented performances that inform and distort current and future perceptions of gay subjectivity. Because TV viewers rely on mediated stereotypes of sexual orientation to fill in the strategic absences, or ambiguities, of a character's presumed sexuality, I also consider the ways in which audience members cited tropes of gay representation to narratize my sexual identity, regardless of how I acted on the show. I analyze fan-generated messages left at one of *Big Brother*'s most active viewer forums, SurvivorSucks. com. I use spectator commentary in this chapter to triangulate my autoethnographic observations and theorize how some audience members interpreted my character.

The Trope of the Crying Gay Man

Being there. July 15, 2010

Twenty-one days ago, we entered the house; and 25 days ago I promised entertainment reporters that I would not spend time in the house crying like previous gay *Big Brother* contestants. "I won't be a big gay cry baby, like Bunky from Season 2," I pledged. These words echo in my ear as I participate in the season's first endurance competition, which will determine the summer's third HoH. We balance our weight on shifting mechanical surfboards as a stream of cold water falls on our heads and large industrial-sized fans cough frigid air on our bodies.

Ten minutes into the competition, *Big Brother* host Julie Chen's voice booms over loudspeakers in the backyard and announces that the first five people to fall off their surfboards will not have food, sleep, or hot water restrictions for the week, meaning second through fifth place competitors will be the week's "have-nots." "So, basically, the people who suck in this competition are rewarded for poor performance and the people who excel are punished," I note. Only two options are available to houseguests who want to avoid have-not punishments: throw the competition by jumping off the apparatus, or be the last person standing and win Head of Household. The HoH never has food, sleep, or water restrictions.

Only minutes after Julie makes her announcement, several people fall off their surfboards, until only four players remain. The final four competitors include Matt, my closest friend in the house; Andrew, a divorced father; Brendon, a man involved in the first "showmance" of our season; and me.

When trying to stay on a competition apparatus, it has become customary for competitors in *Big Brother* endurance challenges to reference loved ones. Today's competition is no different. Matt repeatedly claims that he is "doing it" for his wife Stacy. Andrew periodically yells out "Gila," the name of his daughter. Brendon perseveres because winning the challenge is the only way he can guarantee that Rachel, his love interest on the show, will survive one more week.

I cannot help but notice the extent to which my opponents' self-encouragement is grounded in performative enactments of heteronormativity, in which my participation is, at best, constrained and, at worst, not allowed. Unlike Matt, I live in a state where I am not legally allowed to marry. Unlike Andrew, my sex acts are not procreative, and I do not have the financial resources to acquire a child by way of unconventional methods. Unlike Brendon, I was not put in the house with "showmance" opportunities, let alone six potential romantic partners. I endure the admittedly ridiculous elements of the surfboard competition "for" my recently deceased father, whatever "for" might mean.

As my size-eight feet struggle to stay on the surfboard, I remember the last line of the letter my father wrote me after I told him that I was gay. He said, "I will always try to find the wisdom to guide you through stormy seas which lay ahead, the compassion to understand who you are, and the love to be at your side when the world seems heartless to you." Gallons of near-glacial water pouring on my head mask tears that tango down my cheeks; tears that, 25 days ago, I promised I would not cry; tears that performatively enact the trope of a crying gay man.

More than two hours into the competition and only Matt and I remain on our surfboards. Jumping off the surfboard early in the game would have guaranteed the comforts of food and hot water, but here I stand and shiver. I have something to prove to the little boy inside of me, the one who kids chased across the school football field, as they screamed, "Die, fag!" My childhood was an exercise in endurance. I withstand the elements in part because I do not want to be "that gay," the weak one, the "faggot" who is unwilling to endure. I playfully and triumphantly announce to the cameras, "This is for all the bullshit I had to endure in high school." Most of my roommates respond by cheering me on and laughing.

Masculine bravado aside, I have to make an important strategic decision. Is it more important for me to win an endurance competition and prove my strength or lay low and improve my chances of making it to the end of the game? If I throw the competition, Matt will become HoH and will have to select two houseguests for eviction. Feeling safe from possible elimination due to my close friendship with Matt, I jump off the surfboard and let him get proverbial blood on his hands. Have-not restrictions begin the minute my feet leave the surfboard. I walk into the kitchen, where I see the five poorest performing participants gobble up warm pizza, crack beers, and discuss the competition.

"Wow, Ragan! I didn't expect you to last as long as you did," Andrew exclaims. "You really impressed me."

For the next hour, Andrew repeatedly tells me that he can't believe how well I performed in the endurance challenge. I wonder why he is surprised. I feel like his repeated and, as I read them, backhanded, belittling compliments have something to do with my sexuality. I, of course, may use a history of homophobic abuse to narratize, or fill in the missing blanks of our interaction.

I finally make my way to the have-not bedroom, where I find my new bed for the week: a broken pool lounger. Take second in the endurance competition → have-not. Growing up gay, I am intimately familiar with the cruel repetition of not having.

Prom → have-not, cannot bring a boy as my date. Equal rights → have-not, cannot marry in my state. I wallow in self-pity, as I reflect on a life that seems trapped on the wrong side of the "→," a one-way flow that paints me as subhuman, less than, and in a perpetual state of having not.

In my life outside of the *Big Brother* house, I turn to poetry and scholarship to work my way out of self-indulgent moments, put things into perspective, and remind myself of all the things I do, in fact, have. *Big Brother* is designed to keep me in a frenzied emotional state. I am currently undergoing torture in its most literal sense. I consume fewer than 500 calories a day, when average adults typically

58 Fagan: Awesome Representative

require 2000; am sleep-deprived; cannot use hot water; am taken away from and not allowed to communicate with anyone I love; and am not permitted to read and write. So I cry. I cry like I did the day my father died. I cry until my eyes burn and turn a rich crimson. I bawl until thick strands of snot clog my nose. And with each tear I become the very character I promised I would not portray. To modify Descartes, I cry, therefore I am gay.

Being here

Almost everyone in the *Big Brother 12* house cried, but, by the time I was evicted, production featured crying as one of my defining characteristics. In the final have-not challenge of the season, we played a game of bluff, where the remaining contestants drank shots, and our opponents had to guess whether we consumed a tasty or revolting blended beverage. Fake tears filled my eyes each time I revealed my poker face. My roommates, who narrated the scene, highlighted how my performance of crying in the have-not competition had become a definitive characteristic of my persona. Matt claimed that, "Ragan just went total theatre queen: big, flamboyant, dramatic, crying and whining the whole time." "What's new," described Hayden, *Big Brother 12*'s eventual winner, "Ragan's crying. He's been crying for the past two or three weeks. Why stop now?" A year after the finale, Hayden admitted to me that a member of production prompted him to make the connection between my fake tears in the shots game and more genuine instances of crying in the house.

Commentary on my crying did not end in the house. E!'s pop culture show *The Soup* featured a clip from *Big Brother 12*, in which I sat alone in a hammock and cried to a sock puppet designed to resemble me. As tears glazed my face, I whimpered to the sock puppet and said, "Rough day." The camera then cut to the puppet on my hand, as its mouth quivered and appeared to mimic my sobs. In this "pornography of emotion,"[23] tears are a part of my behavior meant to represent the whole of my character. Tears provide the proof of the truth of gay stereotypes, namely that gay men are weak and less than men. My tears were symbolically more potent than two second-place finishes in endurance competitions, where, in both contests, I lasted longer than a Texas Tech football player and Arizona State University baseball player, nicknamed Beast and Animal respectively.

"Flamboyant," "flaming," and "overly emotional" gay men affirm hegemonic masculinity by representing what masculinity is not, namely demonstrative about feelings.[24] Crying gay men are the have-nots of masculinity. The catch is that gender in this scenario affirms a synecdochical relationship, wherein gendered behavior is a part of identity that stands in for the whole of sexuality, despite the fact that gender and sexuality are distinct categories. Those who performatively enact heteronormative masculinity are expected to repress all emotions with the exception of anger.[25] Other emotional displays might be used to critique a person's character, where "character" represents both my character on the show and heterosexual ethos, or heteronormative credibility. In the absence of gay sex acts, tears synecdochically represented the whole of my sexuality in the *Big Brother* house.

The Trope of the Gay Villain

Season 12 was dubbed *Big Brother's* "Season of Sabotage." Upon moving into the house, Julie Chen announced that one of the contestants was a saboteur. "Their mission is to sabotage your game and wreak as much havoc as possible. This person can sabotage an individual, a group, or all of you." In the game's first week, we had to operate under the assumption that each contestant was the saboteur and any information we shared with him or her might be used to impair our game.

The only place I felt like I could have an earnest conversation was the *Big Brother* Diary Room. Almost every day, a deep man's voice commanded each houseguest to, "Please come to the Diary Room." When called to the Diary Room, a contestant walks to a black door in the living room and presses a silver button that alerts production. A member of the production team unlocks the door, allowing the houseguest to walk down a thin, dark hallway to another door that is the confessional's entrance. The Diary Room is a small, black rectangular box that contains a love seat, two cameras, and a microphone. The cameras allow *Big Brother's* team to talk to and record contestants without any of us seeing producers. Each week, cast members spend hours in the Diary Room responding to producers' questions. Story supervisors carefully edit our answers and use them to create a narrative for the program. The storytelling we provide walks audience members through the rules and mechanics of weekly competitions, alliance formations and breakdowns, and a range of other mundane happenings. The Diary Room, or "DR," is the only place in the house the audience cannot access when viewing the show's Internet live feed. My first month in the game, the DR provided a safe space for me to vent frustrations, discuss strategy, and seek emotional support.

I slowly learned that the confessional is also the area where members of production influence houseguests' opinions of one another and manipulate contestant behavior. My first indication that producers use the DR to influence the game came in the first week. Head of Household Hayden nominated a Las Vegas VIP waitress named Rachel and a tall, muscular swimming instructor named Brendon for eviction. The two became easy targets after they formed a showmance, or romantic pairing, in the game's first week. Many of us suspected that Brendon might be the saboteur because he was one of three contestants who went missing when the saboteur pulled a prank on our first night in the house. Brendon's budding romance and suspect whereabouts during the game's initial act of sabotage made him an idea candidate for our first eviction. The house's plans to evict Brendon deteriorated after he won the Power of Veto competition and took himself "off the chopping block," or vetoed his nomination.

60 Fagan: Awesome Representative

Brendon's move forced Hayden to name a replacement nominee. Hayden decided to name the house's sole bisexual player Annie as the replacement nominee. Annie was one of the most liked players in the house but she had formed alliances with many houseguests only days into the game. Like Brendon, Annie was also unaccounted for during one of the saboteur's first prank, leading some of us to wonder if she was the villain Julie Chen warned us about on our first night. Before the Head of Household announces the names of his or her nominees or replacement nominee, he or she goes to the Diary Room and talks about his or her rationale with members of production. Editors use bits and pieces of the HoH's strategizing in CBS broadcasts to help contextualize his or her decision.

After Hayden named Annie as his replacement nominee, we had a conversation where he revealed that members of production pressured him to keep Annie off the chopping block. "Why would you want to get rid of Annie?" I imagine a producer asking Hayden. "She likes you, Hayden. Why not go after somebody who is more of a threat?" The more production tried to get Annie out of Hayden's crosshairs, the more suspicious he became of the men and women talking to him in the Diary Room. Hayden's logic made sense. If Annie were the saboteur, producers would certainly try to keep her in the game. Annie leaving in the first week would totally dismantle Season 12's sabotage-themed twist. Hayden's concerns of production manipulation were substantiated three days after Annie's eviction when we learned that she was in fact the saboteur.

In week five, production discovered a clever way to reintroduce the saboteur theme into the game. Julie Chen announced that viewers would have an opportunity to vote on one of the remaining players to become the new saboteur. The houseguest with the most votes would be called to the Diary Room and offered the role. In exchange for two weeks of sabotaging other players, the houseguest would win $20,000. Much to my surprise and eventual chagrin, U.S. viewers voted for me to become the season's second saboteur.

The saboteur role extends a history of gay antagonists in film and television. Media critics have documented how gay, lesbian, and bisexual characters tend to be depicted as villains on television[26] and in Disney movies,[27] witches and psychos in canonical films,[28] and perverts and child molesters in the news.[29] Not surprisingly, both production and viewers cast the only gay and lesbian characters in Season 12 as villains. By definition, we had to disrupt gameplay and antagonize our roommates. Homosexuality has been used throughout TV history to "establish an additional level of deviance for [villainous] characters."[30] Annie and I, like so many gay and lesbian characters before us, were situated as "a problem disrupting heterosexuals' lives and expectations"[31] and an "evil to be destroyed."[32] Everyone in the house knew about the saboteur and wanted him or her gone, but none of the contestants knew his or her identity.

Most of my saboteur duties involved simple and silly pranks, like hiding a note that read, "I know your secret," under a competitor's pillow. Despite the saboteur's frivolity, playing the role augmented my feelings of isolation. I was not allowed to tell any of my allies that I was the person responsible for shenanigans that kept everyone up at night. Many of my roommates began to target my allies in the house as the saboteur, and I certainly did not want to be responsible for a friend's eviction. I walked around the house in a perpetual state of guilt and shame. Each time production called me into the diary room and asked me to perform a task, I cried. After successfully completing two weeks of sabotage, I was awarded $20,000. By the end of my villainous stint, *Entertainment Weekly* dubbed me *Big Brother 12*'s "sob-oteur."

Many fans of the show rightfully complained that I was not a very exciting saboteur but found other aspects of my character to vilify. Part-for-the-whole relationships—between tears and character, and one gay man and the entire gay community—may be used to help interpret a viewer's process of narratization. Anticipations of how gay characters should or typically act on a reality program limit and enable a viewer's perception of who I was on *Big Brother*, even when my performance of self-disavowed expectations.

To demonstrate how some viewers relied on tropes of gay representation to narratize my character, I entered a world that producers, casting directors, and the show psychologist beg *Big Brother* participants not to visit: *Big Brother* fan Web sites. Several fan bulletin board contributors are especially brutal in their assessments of *Big Brother* houseguests. Fan commentary on the Internet tends to take a particularly nasty turn when viewers discuss contestants who come from historically marginalized groups. Nowhere did homophobic rhetoric emerge more salient than in the *Survivor* Sucks community, a fan forum that proudly flames or makes fun of reality show participants. The tone of the board is dark, mean-spirited, and sarcastic. *Survivor* Sucks members titled the discussion thread about my character, "Fagan: 'Awesome' Representative of the Gay Community." Viewers in the thread refer to my character as "Crygan"[33] and "Ragonorrhea,"[34] and say things like, "Fagan HATE! Die, motherfucker!"[35] and "DIE FAG!"[36]

Explicit homophobic messages are mixed in with statements of support for my character and a few posts that bemoan the amplified and unapologetic homophobia espoused by many of the forum's contributors. Other viewers justify their homophobic behavior by suggesting that gay characters on *Big Brother* are bad representatives of the gay community. FLgirl writes, "I love the gays, but why do 99% of the gay guys they have on BB suck?!"[37] Some members of the forum self-identify as gay when rationalizing their own anti-gay hate speech. Fisherman39 writes, "Most of the guys posting Fagan hate are gay anyways, so we can use the word fag all we want. Ragan is the true definition of a fag."[38] Similarly, Xreality-dotnet claims that, "As a gay guy, I condone all use of the word 'fag' to describe Ragan."[39]

Gay bashing on the site also takes pictorial form. The *Survivor* Sucks fan forum includes a "photochops" thread where some of the board's more creative members use software called Photoshop to alter, manipulate, and "chop" images of *Big Brother* cast members. Fans who modified my images tended to narratize a sex life for my character. Jaynes explains that people narratize others, as much as they do the "I." "A stray fact," he argues, "is narratized to fit with some other stray fact. A child cries in the street and we narratize the event into a mental picture of a lost child and a parent searching for it."[40] Narratization allows a *Big Brother* viewer to fill in missing blanks when he or she perceives that there is more to a situation, scene, or character than what is shown in a broadcast.

In the absence of my character performing gay sex acts on the show, some fans relied on tropes of gay representation to narratize what they assumed to be my essential characteristics. In other words, they creatively rendered aspects of my sexuality that were absent from *Big Brother* broadcasts. Before the show even premiered, members of *Survivor* Sucks altered my pictures and both pictorially and verbally narratized what they perceived to be my sexual proclivities. ArtMaggot posted Figure 3.1 to the *Survivor* Sucks "Official Photochops Thread" on July 3, which was five days *before* the premiere of *Big Brother 12*. In Figure 3.1, the viewer placed my head over a gay porn actor, who is anally penetrating another man. *Big Brother 12* houseguest Enzo's face is positioned on top of the penetrated actor. The photo's caption reads, "How to tame a Stallion [sic]"; "stallion" is most likely a synecdochical reference to Enzo's Italian heritage (i.e., "Italian stallion"), and my gayness is presumably what "tames" him.

ArtMaggot uploaded Figure 3.2 to the site on July 7, one day before the first episode. Figure 3.2, "The Ass Whisperer," features my CBS press photo backdropped by a larger-than-life butt with a screaming mouth transposed over the anus. In both photographs, ArtMaggot narratizes my character by focusing on what he may assume is the most significant characteristic of my identity as a gay man: anal sex. These images demonstrate how some viewers infused my character with sexuality, even when they were not exposed to gay sex acts, or, at that particular time, any of my behaviors.

Other Photoshopped images in the *Survivor* Sucks forum reference viral and predatory tropes of gay representation. Many of these pictures humorously call attention to my friendship with Matt Hoffman, *Big Brother* 12's self-proclaimed "diabolical super genius." Our roommates and members of production joked that we had developed a "showmance," or romantic pairing. *Big Brother* 12 contestant Andrew read our relationship as queer in the first week of the game. After production suggested that two people in the house were lifelong friends, Andrew went into the diary room and claimed, "From the beginning, I thought Matt and Ragan [were the secret friends]. I think Matt is gay, and I think them two are in a relationship." Andrew narrated a sexual component to my friendship with Matt and then narrated his theory in the season's third episode.

Hints of my sexuality infecting Matt took center stage in episode 20. Matt admitted to two other houseguests that he had a dream about Hayden, a hunky, young Arizona State University baseball player. "I dreamt about shirtless Hayden," he confessed.

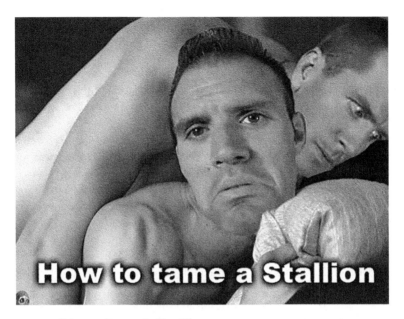

FIGURE 3.1 "How to Tame a Stallion"[41]

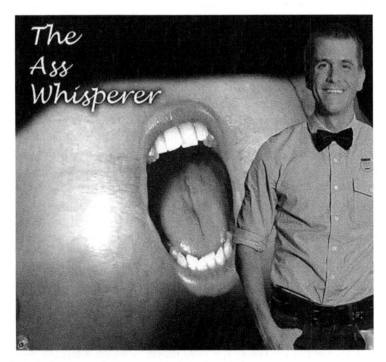

FIGURE 3.2 Ragan as "The Ass Whisperer"[42]

"With no shirt on," asked Lane, an oilrig salesman and former Texas Tech football player. Later, in a diary room confession, Lane stated, "In Texas, if you do have a dream like that, you do not tell anyone."

The gay contagion sequence ends with a diary room segment featuring Matt, who joked, "This place is crazy. It messes with your mind. I'm in some homosexual showmance. And now I'm dreaming about shirtless Hayden."

Our close relationship was performatively constructed as Matt's downfall in the game. "Matty's getting too close to Ragan," Enzo claimed only days before he devised a plan to evict Matt. Enzo's heteronormative narratization is par for the course in television, where homosexuality is regularly presented as an obstacle for heterosexual characters. Battles and Hilton-Morrow argue that when a "program explicitly deals with the question of sexuality, it falls back on the convention of treating homosexuality as a problem, especially for straight characters in the narrative."[43] On August 26, 2010, Enzo's plan came to fruition, and Matt was eliminated from the competition. In a post-eviction interview, he sat across from Julie Chen, who grilled him about our friendship and the Brigade, a secret all-male alliance of which I was not a member.

"I was hovering between the Brigade and my little showmance," he quipped. The live studio audience seated behind Matt and Julie chuckled.

Julie continued, "You and Ragan were best friends in the house. Why didn't you tell him about your [other] alliance? Why did you 'throw him under the bus?'"

"Ragan's my little boy toy," he replied. As if cued by a placard, the audience once again laughed. "It was a matter of playing with my heart or my head. My heart was with Ragan but my head was with the Brigade."

By the time Matt was evicted from the house, audience members had grown accustomed to laughing at suggestions that our friendship was more than platonic. Production sanitized the joke of our "showmance" by featuring clips of and repeated references to Matt's wife. The comedy of our friendship functions as "antirhetoric," or discourse that "simultaneously promotes and disavows itself—renouncing its intent even as it amuses audiences and advances agendas."[44] The "straight-mistaken-for-gay trope" is commonplace in television and "derives much of its humor from the audience's knowledge that the character(s) is/are not in fact gay."[45] My homosocial relationship with Matt may have been palatable to some viewers, because our coupling constituted a performative enactment of gay subjectivity without Matt ever having to "go gay" in the house.

My friendship with Matt became a popular topic of conversation among viewers, some of whom used their Photoshop skills to narratize the assumed missing elements of our "gay" relationship. EgregiousPhilbin referenced tropes of gay predators when he reworked the film poster for *Single White Female* so that it pictorially depicts a narratized interpretation of my friendship with Matt (see Figure 3.3). *Single White Female* is a 1992 movie in which a bisexual sociopath

FIGURE 3.3 "Single White Shemale"[46]

obsesses over, stalks, and brutalizes her roommate. The image includes a transphobic and homophobic play on the movie's title, wherein EgregiousPhilbin trades "female" for "shemale." Shemale is sometimes used to describe transgender women in the sex-trade industry. Many trans people find the term offensive. EgregiousPhilbin's comedic rendition of the movie poster also features a collage of four photos strategically placed to make it seem as though I am secretly staring at and of course crying over Matt. The image cites and repeats myths that suggest gay men are predators, especially in their relationships with heterosexual men. The doctored photographs also play into a troupe of gay psychosis, where gay men are depicted as mentally ill, desperate, and lonely—compulsively sabotaging all things "pure" and "good."

Despite fan narratization, I was particularly careful not to come off as a sex-starved gay predator. In the first week of the game, diary room producers regularly asked me to describe male contestants in sexual terms. They wanted to know if I found any of the men in the house hot.

"Sure, Hayden is cute," I replied.

Questions about attraction quickly devolved into probes about potential sex acts. Did I want to make out with Hayden? What would I like to do to Hayden? I told the producer that I did not feel comfortable sexualizing the male houseguests, most of whom were the age of my undergraduate students. The production team quickly learned that I would not "go there," so, after the first week, they stopped asking me about in-house desire. Fans of the show, in turn, filled the void.

Each of the aforementioned photos references tropes of gay men, even when certain motifs were absent in *Big Brother 12*. Fan-produced images display the reiterative force of gay stereotypes. I never had sex on the show, nor did I fall in love with a straight man. Some viewers, nevertheless, narratized an explicit and hypersexual story for me. When looked at through a lens of narratization, character production is not simply a matter of representation. Character production also entails a complex process of perception. Residual understandings and protentional anticipations of gay subjectivity constrain and enable who gay characters on reality television may be/come. Tropes work in an interconnected web that trapped me, anticipated my actions, and narratized my defining characteristics and behaviors. Production helped facilitate this process, as did audience members. These tropes were entrenched and reproduced, even as I actively worked to resist them.

The Trope of the Flaming Homosexual

George Chauncey places the "flaming faggot" in the same web of association as feminizing tropes of homosexuality that emerged in the early twentieth century, including the gender invert, queen, "she-man, nance, and sissy."[47] "Flaming" is a term typically reserved for gay men who dress and/or behave in an effeminate, dramatic, or flamboyant manner. A flaming homosexual typically speaks in a high pitch and with a lisp, uses female pronouns when referencing himself and other men, and wears bright, sometimes feminine clothing.

In his ethnographic study of gay culture in the U.S. Midwest, Joseph Goodwin notes that flaming queens are often ostracized by other gay men "since many gays feel that such people are 'politically incorrect,' reinforcing straights' stereotypes of gays and thereby hindering the cause of gay liberation."[48] Anti-femme sentiment within the gay community may be partially attributed to the flaming queen's ubiquity in mass media. Featuring a flamboyant gay man on a television show enables media executives to create an illusion of inclusivity. A gay man so undeniably queer in his mannerisms never has to prove his sexuality by having sex, or engaging in any sexual behavior that might offend mainstream audiences. The flamer's symbolic impotence may explain why he is mass media's primary go-to motif of queer representation.

Examples of the trope include two snapping queens of color named Blaine and Antoine on *In Living Color*'s popular "Men on Films" sketch; hypersexual and perpetually energized Jack on *Will and Grace*; colorfully dressed Stanford Blatch on *Sex and the City*; and Kurt on *Glee*, whose father once described as so gay he "sings like Diana Ross" and dresses like he owns a "magical chocolate factory." Flaming queens are as popular on reality TV programs as they are sitcoms. In his study of gay characters on *Survivor*, *Big Brother*, and *Pop Idol*, Christopher Pullen notes that gay participants are often "selected for performing, and adhering to, recognized dramatic traits associated with stereotypical gay performance."[49]

Pullen's findings unfortunately focus single-mindedly on enactments of gay representation and ignore perhaps the most critical component of stereotypes: perception. Stereotypes say more about the people who use them to interpret behavior than they do the people they aim to represent. Confirmation bias based on stereotypes shapes the way people—gay and straight—view sexual minorities.[50] Television viewers are culturally predisposed to pay selective attention to moments in which a gay character performs "dramatic traits associated with stereotypical behaviors." But, of greater consequence, most of the U.S. audience is programmed to interpret even the most humdrum behavior of gay men as excessively gay and the proof of gay stereotypes. Stereotypes, in this context, are more a performative enactment of a viewer's reductive understanding of sexual minorities than a reflection of any LGBTQ character. As a mode of media criticism, performative spectatorship is designed to interrogate the ways in which patterns of representation are also patterns of reception.

Fans in message forums often narratized, or de/coded, my behavior as flaming. A *Survivor* Sucks contributor named Archimedes for example digitally manipulated a photo of *The Fantastic Four*, a super-hero action movie based on a comic book (see Figure 3.4). Each of the four houseguests in the picture shares traits of the comic book hero on which he or she has been transposed. Former Texas Tech football player Lane's face is pasted on the Thing's body. In the comic, the Thing is a rock-like humanoid that possesses superhuman strength. Twenty-four-year-old boutique manager Kristen's face is placed over the Invisible Woman. A speech bubble reading "time to disappear" hovers over Kristen's head. Kristen's caption is especially fitting given that Archimedes created the image the week Kristen was targeted for eviction. The group's scientific genius, Mr. Fantastic, is represented by Brendon, the only man in the house with an advanced degree in science. My head sits atop the Human Torch's body. The Human Torch's catchphrase "flame on"

68 Fagan: Awesome Representative

FIGURE 3.4 "Flame on!" From left to right: Ragan as the Human Torch, Lane as the Thing, Kristen as the Invisible Woman, and Brendon as Mr. Fantastic[51]

is placed to the right of my face. Archimedes's suggestion is that I am a flaming homosexual. Members of *Survivor* Sucks began to suggest I was a flamer several days before CBS's premiere of Season 12. Working off little more information than my text-based profile posted at CBS.com (see Figure 3.5), viewers like OttoJr surmised that my life "seemed to revolve around being gay. Leave first, please."[52] The profile with which OttoJr takes issue contains few references to my sexuality. Only four of my character summary's 306 words reference my sexuality. The profile overwhelmingly focuses on my career, take on past seasons of *Big Brother*, and general life philosophies. Minimal references to my sexuality are enough for readers like OttoJr to conclude that 1) my life revolves around being gay, and as a result 2) I should be the first person evicted from the house. Another board member named WylDog emphatically replies, "A-fucking-MEN! You just pin pointed [sic] the exact reason I usually don't like flaming gays as a general rule. I can't stand those whom everything they say/do/breathe has to remind you that they're gay."[53] Again, OttoJr and WylDog make these statements before even witnessing my on-show comportment.

Other members of *Survivor Sucks* liken me to other flamboyant, or flaming, gay sidekicks on television, like Jack on *Will and Grace*. Figure 3.6 is a picture of my face Photoshopped on Jack's body. Earthdog created the image several days prior to *Big Brother 12*'s premiere, indicating that fans of the show used gay stereotypes to read my character before they witnessed me interact with anyone on the program.

Fagan: "Awesome" Representative of the Gay Community. He's made us SO....

Name: Ragan Fox
Age: 34
Current Residence: West Hollywood, Calif.
Occupation: College Professor
Three adjectives that describe you: Funny, genuine, intelligent
Favorite Activities: Writing and performing poetry. My podcast is my biggest hobby. The show features my comedic take on pop culture and politics. I discuss everything on it.
What do you think will be the most difficult part about living inside the Big Brother house: There is a lot of fighting and I tend to hold a grudge.
Strategy for winning Big Brother: Don't rock the boat until I have to. Float until war is declared and the floaters align with strong players who are perceived to be bigger threats. Form a secret alliance about two weeks into the game. Don't win too many competitions but don't obviously throw them.
What types of people would you NOT choose to live with you in the house: Homophobes, 18-23 year-olds (the ages of students I teach), ultra conservatives
A recurring theme on Big Brother is "expect the unexpected." How would you handle "the unexpected:" I'd roll with the punches.
Which past Big Brother cast member did you like most or least: Most: Janelle, because what you saw is what you got. Least; Boogie. White rappers are too much of a paradox for me. And Chima, she was a poor sport and bad game player.
What are you afraid of: Heights, flying, homophobia
What is the accomplishment you are most proud of: I've had 2 poetry collections published: Heterophobia and Exile in Gayville
Finish this sentence: "My life's motto is:" The Golden Rule: Treat others how you want/expect to be treated.
Is there anything else you want to tell the audience about yourself: I love to make people laugh. In my world, there's nothing a well-placed fart joke can't cure. Humor is how I roll with the punches.

FIGURE 3.5   My CBS profile reposted on *Survivor Sucks* several days before the *Big Brother 12* premiere[54]

70 Fagan: Awesome Representative

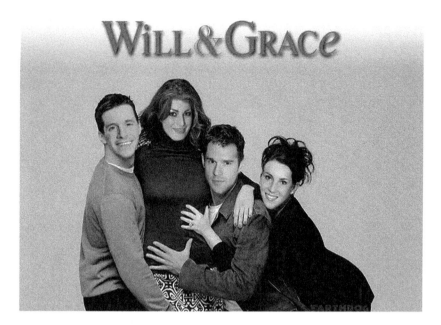

FIGURE 3.6 Ragan as the flaming gay sidekick[55]

A homophobic, flaming-oriented pattern of viewer interpretation emerges when reading *Survivor Sucks* comment threads about previous gay contestants. I was only able to locate fan forums dedicated to houseguests dating back to the program's seventh season. Gay men on *Big Brother* represent a wide range of demographics, yet many audience members rely on reductive flaming stereotypes of homosexuality when narratizing them. Take, for example, the following pieces of fan commentary about gay contestants:

- Regarding Season 3 and Season 7's Marcellas, a 36-year-old Black man in the entertainment industry, Karen1407 types, "I can't stand this flaming whore!"[56] Cuauhtemoc Cosby writes a post addressed to Marcellas that reads, "You are a useless man whore, you stupid fuck face flaming shit."[57]
- Regarding Season 8's Dustin, a 22-year-old White shoe salesman, Tritonsrod says, "I hate this flamer,"[58] and Nomiiiii describes him as "mildly hot" but "totally flaming."[59] Tronajmaaaaan argues that Dustin is "way more flaming and stereotypical than [his ex-boyfriend] Joe. I hate when people tell him how masculine and 'non-gay' he is."[60] JesusofNajareth celebrated Dustin's eviction by writing, "Ding, dong, the flaming gonorrhea-infested, unsanitary, walking petri dish queen bitch is gone."

- Regarding Season 9's Joshua, a 25-year-old White man in advertising, Dav-eSoGay says, "Josh makes fun of the way people look. Pretty crazy coming from a fat, flaming queen who looks ten years older than he actually is."[61] ScruffyGuy complains, "Joshua, you are without a doubt the single most sickening piece of garbage to ever 'represent' gay people on reality television. Do you think for one moment that Mommy and Daddy didn't know you were a flaming, wretched queen every time you flounced into a room?"[62]
- Regarding Season 11's Kevin, a 29-year old biracial graphic designer, Daguerreo proclaims, "Kevin is not representative of me or any gay person I know. Go down in flames, you flaming queen! Die in a fire!"[63] LoungeAct types, "Hate! Hate! Hate! That spineless pussy Kevin makes even a flaming queen like [*Big Brother 11* houseguest] Ronnie look like Chuck Norris!"[64]
- Regarding Season 14's Wil, a 24-year-old White man in marketing, Buttsecks chastises, "No offense *Big Brother*, but get some gay guy next season whose voice isn't so high and whose hobbies don't include dress-up and watching Lady GaGa videos."[65] SurvivorNinja shares, "I really wanted a hot straight-acting gay guy this season. Since *Big Brother* doesn't cast men like that, I will happily settle for this drag queen mess."[66]
- Regarding Season 15's winner Andy, a 26-year-old White college adjunct instructor, Riff comments, "I'm astounded he even has students. If I was in a school where they gave me *that* for a teacher, I'd go directly to administration and drop the class. I wouldn't have a flamer for a teacher. I'd never be able to take them seriously."[67]
- Regarding Season 16's Frankie, a 31-year-old Latino, Riff once again writes, "He is narcissistic, self-centered, histrionic, smarmy, condescending, slimy, skeevy, AIDS-infested, foul, repulsive, noxious, flaming, irritating, nasty, boring and boorish . . . and those are his good traits."[68]
- Regarding Season 18's Jozea, a 25-year-old Latino makeup artist, Sardoni-callyIrrelevant muses, "Robyn Kass must have an agenda to destroy the gay rights movement. It's the only explanation for the repulsive queens she churns out year after year."[69] Moovivor guesses, "I'm 150–200% sure he's a flaming homosexual and dancing around the label."[70] The viewer's presumption was based on Jozea's textual profile posted on CBS.com. The profile makes no mention of Jozea's sexuality.

The age, race, profession, and mannerisms of *Big Brother*'s gay houseguests change from season to season. The one thing that remains constant, though, is how many audience members interpret gay men on the program. Performative spectatorship calls our attention to the ways in which the flaming stereotype is largely centered around perceptions of homosexuality. Repetition is a key aspect of gender performativity. Butler contends that, "Performativity must be understood not as a singular or deliberative 'act,' but, rather, as the reiterative and citational practice by which discourse produces the effects that it names."[71] Viewers repeatedly coding gay houseguests as "flaming" reveal the reiterative, world-creating force of gay stereotypes, along with the "exclusionary matrix by which [heterosexual] subjects are formed" and celebrated.[72]

Borrowing from Butler, Adi Kuntsman frames flaming as performative practices that "constitute the very subjects they aim to wound or protect."[73] Unlike the previously discussed modes of gay representation, flaming characterizes an amalgamation of characteristics. Four traits performatively engender the flaming homosexual trope. Flaming gays tend to be 1) feminine, 2) hypersexual, 3) overdramatic, and 4) masters of witty insults.

Flaming as Femme

Flaming is associated with feminine performances of gay male subjectivity. Numerous Photoshopped images on *Survivor Sucks* play into the flaming homosexual trope by pictorially representing me in women's garb. Figure 3.7 is a digitally manipulated image in which UNCDavid places me in a dress, makes fun of Matt's height, and jokes about Brendon's poor sportsmanship after losing endurance competitions to me and Matt. The irony is that the viewer's fan art suggests that Matt and I lack masculinity (i.e., Matt's short stature and my perceived femininity) but also acknowledges that we placed first and second respectively in two strength-based endurance competitions. The implication is that despite whatever masculine feats I may accomplish, I am still little more than a man in a dress. Earthdog provides another pictorial connection between the trope of the flaming homosexual and femininity. In Figure 3.8, Earthdog Photoshops my face onto a poster for the play *Sunset Boulevard*. Earthdog also cites tropes of gay psychosis in his rendering of my character. My head sits atop the body of Norma Desmond, the play's mentally ill, suicidal, and murderous main character. Figures 3.7 and 3.8 function as "ascribed femmephobia" that draws on "cultural associations of feminine subordination as a tool to 'demote' the target."[74] Femme theorist Rhea Hoskin argues that ascribed femmephobia is a "process of gendering, which denotes inferiority by making use of the subordinated status of femininity."[75]

Anti-femme pile-on mentality continues throughout my *Survivor Sucks* thread. User KudrowFan implores, "Add me to the list of people who want a masculine gay guy on next season. Enough with the stereotypical feminine guys."[78] Xanster82 writes, "Fagan is making such a bad name for us normal gays. It's definitely time for a masculine gay next season."[79] Only two seasons prior, *Big Brother's* cast included a gay bull rider from Dallas named Steven Daigle, a man whose profession and gender performance meet many traits associated with hegemonic masculinity. *Big Brother* has cast of diverse group of gay men, including Caucasians, Latinos, and African Americans. Gay houseguests have worked in a range of professions, from rodeo performance and technical writing to education and advertising. Some *Big Brother* gays speak in higher pitches and lilting cadences,

FIGURE 3.7 Ragan in a dress after coming in second place in two endurance competitions[76]

other's talk in a lower register. Some dress in vibrant colors and unconventional, feminine clothing (e.g., summer scarves and deep v-neck shirts), others don drab, beige clothes one might find at a suburban barbecue. Viewers like KudrowFan and Xanster82 are culturally trained to only recognize a gay character as gay when he breaks codes of hegemonic masculinity. Their confirmation bias is so sharply tuned that even a momentary breach of masculine norms is enough to assert the

74 Fagan: Awesome Representative

FIGURE 3.8 Ragan as Norma Desmond[77]

viewers' femmephobic misconception that the same sort of gay is always included on the series, despite the gay cast's diversity in race, ethnicity, social class, manners of speech, and professions. Most seasons, viewers in fan forums bemoan that the season's gay character is little more than a stereotype. Femme-bashing is then justified as an appropriate response to *Big Brother* presumably casting the same type of gay men who give "normal gays" a bad name.

Flaming and the Hyper-sexual Paradox

Flaming is partially characterized by a hyper-sexualization of gay men. The catch is that flaming homosexuals in the media are eroticized in ways that *imply* sexuality without including even the subtlest form of sexual contact. Few television programs have dared to show two or more men in sexually intimate settings. In 1994, for example, producers of the primetime soap opera *Melrose Place* opted to edit out a kiss between two gay characters after conservative organizations threatened to boycott FOX. Cameras pan to a heterosexual character responding to the kiss just before the two men's lips touch. In a season finale that featured multiple illicit storylines, including a father sexually abusing two of his daughters, a man suing his fiancé's daughter for sexual harassment, three women brutally beating a prostitute in a street fight, and a wife purposely running over her husband, news outlets focused myopically on an innocent kiss between two gay characters. The anticipated display of intimacy generated a great deal of publicity for the program and resulted in the series' largest audience: 19.3 million viewers. A similar set of circumstances unfolded on CBS in May of 1994 when *Northern Exposure* featured two gay characters marry without kissing.

Implied acts of homosexual affection on television illustrate one of the primary double-standards of the hetero-/homo-binary—both on and off television. Sexuality tends to only be marked as excessive when performed by a sexual minority. Heterosexual characters on *Melrose Place* sexually abuse one another, engage in acts of prostitution, sleep with one another's in-laws, and have sex in a range of public settings but network executives only cut away from the scene when two gay men kiss. The irony is that censoring displays of homosexual intimacy generate more discourse about homosexuality than they repress. Michel Foucault's repressive hypothesis helps explicate this paradox of censorship. Foucault argues that attempts to block talk about or displays of sexuality have resulted in a "countereffect, a valorization and intensification of indecent speech; an institutional incitement to speak about [sex], and to do so more and more."[80] He continues, "What is peculiar to modern societies, in fact, is not that they consigned sex to a shadow existence, but that they dedicated themselves to speaking of it *ad infinitum*, while exploiting it as the secret."[81] Television viewers, for instance, fill in a network's constructed absences, or sex acts that are merely implied.

Some viewers imbued my character with sexuality, even though I was the only gay man on the twelfth season of *Big Brother* and was the only character denied even the possibility of a romantic coupling. *Survivor* Sucks contributor EgregiousPhilbin references my assumed sexual "fantasy" in his artistic re-rendering of *The Nutty Professor* (see Figure 3.9). The viewer reworks the movie poster so that it reads, "*The Slutty Professor*." My head is superimposed over the body of a mad scientist mixing a potion that will enable me to molest Season 12's male cast members. "What does he become," the poster reads. "What kind of monster?" EgregiousPhilbin perpetuates the myth that all gay men are "hypersexual and

FIGURE 3.9 "Ragan Fox as the Slutty Professor"[83]

unable to control their own desires when they are living in close proximity" to people of the same sex.[82]

Other fan-produced images are more graphic in their sexual displays. Figure 3.10, for instance, is a GIF, or animated image, created by *Big Brother* fan Artmaggot. The GIF begins with a photo of Hayden looking down at his pelvis. A clockwise reading of the photos reveal my head slowly emerge from between Hayden's legs. White fluid symbolizing ejaculate falls from my lips. Artmaggot's suggestion is that I have performed oral sex on Hayden. Since the 1950s, image-based jokes about gay men "focus on oral and anal sex and feminized behavior."[85] In their study of jokes about gays and lesbians, Nardi and Stoller contend that most humor about homosexuality is premised upon debasing gay "men and their masculinity, by making them passive, feminine, or weak, except for their hyper-sexuality."[86]

Flaming Drama Queens Who Know How to Read

I group flaming's last two traits because histrionics and insults often work in conjunction with one another. A gay man's witty jabs often help establish and maintain a dramatic scene. *Big Brother* has featured several moments wherein gay men get fired up (so to speak) and use sharp, sometimes cruel put-downs to eviscerate their opponents. Season 9's Joshua Welch, for example, told fellow contestant Amanda to go hang herself during a verbal altercation. Joshua's words were particularly cruel given that Amanda's father previously committed suicide by hanging himself. After being taunted by fan-favorite Janelle, Season 6's Beau called her a "polyester-hair bitch."

My arguments with flame-haired, super villain Rachel are widely considered the must-see moments of Season 12. I was a top trending topic on social media behemoth Twitter the day I stood up to Rachel. The *New York Post* listed my argument with her as one of the all-time ten best fights in reality TV history. The day after CBS aired my takedown of Rachel, a journalist for the *New York Post* wrote, "I've watched all eleven seasons of *Big Brother* and feel confident saying that last night's fight between Ragan and Rachel is easily the biggest smackdown in the show's history."[87]

Those invested in queer theory and culture might describe my rants as "reading." Reading has two interconnected significations in this context. First, reading characterizes a humorous form of queer invective. The term was popularized in the movie *Paris Is Burning*, where a cast of predominantly Black drag queens incorporated witty, exaggerated insults into their performance. The practice's roots in drag culture illustrate that reading is intimately connected to flamboyant, or flaming, performances of gay subjectivity.

Next, reading more plainly means interpretation, as in, "This is my reading of a particular text." Reading takes on a unique meaning in this book because performative spectatorship blurs the line between writing/performing and reading/

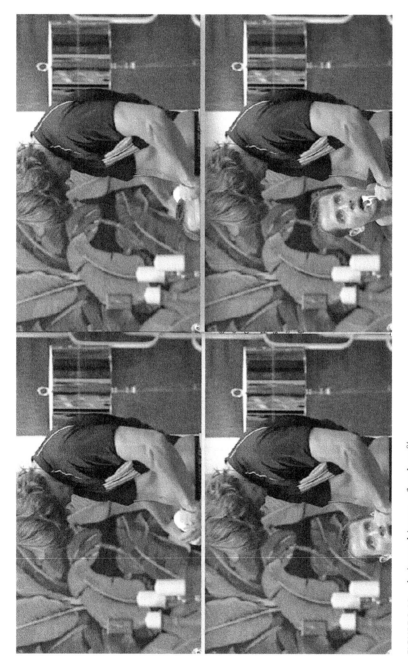

FIGURE 3.10 Animated image of oral sex[84]

audiencing. The queer practice of "reading people to filth" (or harshly criticizing them for a laugh) exemplifies performative spectatorship's dance between reading and performing. The reader uses imagination and creativity to embellish the object of his or her derision and, in doing so, influences how other people may interpret the butt of the speaker's joke.

Reading/interpreting my drama with Rachel requires an appreciation for how production helped cultivate our ire. Twenty-six-year-old Rachel Reilly was, without question, the most audacious person in our cast. "I'm from Vegas. I *am* Vegas," she was fond of saying. A series of hair extensions pulled Rachel's long magenta hair to the middle of her back. Most days in the house, she wore tight micro-dresses, sequins, and dramatic makeup. I marveled at how she gazed into every mirror she passed, which was quite a feat given two-way mirrors adorn *all* walls of the *Big Brother* house. Rachel and I developed a friendship in the first few weeks of the game. We bonded over our mutual love of the camp classic *Showgirls*, admiration of Brendon's chiseled physique, and combined knowledge of *Big Brother* history.

Rachel won several competitions, including the second and fourth Head of Household games. As one of her closest allies, I rarely feared going home in the early weeks of the contest. Rachel's intimate relationship with Brendon, penchant for winning games, and countless arguments with our roommates made her an ideal candidate for eviction. She clashed with nearly every houseguest. Rachel sparred with Annie, Monet, Britney, Hayden, Matt, and even mild-mannered Arkansas police deputy Kathy. Our alliance finally deteriorated in the fifth week of the competition after Matt, my closest friend in the house, won Head of Household and nominated Brendon and Rachel for eviction. Rachel raged after her nomination and suggested I was largely responsible for Matt's decision.

The week leading up to Rachel's eviction was tense. Most of our interactions devolved into arguments. To make matters worse, Brendon worked tirelessly to get the house to evict him instead of Rachel. He began bullying me in the hopes that my contempt for him would eclipse the threat Rachel posed in the game. One afternoon, Brendon lurched close behind me as I walked to the backyard. His large feet stepped on the back of my flip-flops, causing me to stumble. He cursed me out and referred to me as a cockroach. Brendon's bullying only made me more determined to evict Rachel.

The Diary Room also played a hand in my growing disdain for the Vegas cocktail waitress. Producers used my saboteur duties to hint at viewers' contempt for Rachel. *Big Brother's* U.S. audience sent in sabotage suggestions that production shared with me. I had to select one prank from a list of roughly 20 viewer recommendations. The lists often contained several unflattering references to Rachel. One person suggested throwing "Rachel's nasty hair extensions in the pool." Another audience member wanted me to place one of her bikinis in the freezer. Production relied on viewer prompts to build upon the divide in my crumbling

80 Fagan: Awesome Representative

relationship with Rachel and Brendon. Who wants to be associated with a player viewers dislike, especially if she has so many enemies in the house?

Being there. August 14, 2010

Two days ago, Rachel became the fifth person eliminated from the competition and first person sent to the *Big Brother* jury house, where she and the next six evictees will live until the finale and ponder which of the two final players should win the season. The same day we evicted Rachel, Brendon won Head of Household. As the newly minted HoH, Julie allowed him to pick three Have-Nots for the week. Brendon selected the people he found most responsible for Rachel's eviction: me, Britney, and Matt. This is my third time to be a Have-Not, meaning it is the third week my diet will be restricted to *Big Brother* slop, which is basically salty oatmeal. How can I survive another 500-calorie-a-day week? Have-Not food restrictions have already brought me down to 115 pounds of skeletal flesh. "I am down to my birthweight," I joked in the Diary Room.

Yesterday, Brendon nominated me for eviction. I woke up this morning after getting a terrible night's sleep. Production repeatedly called me into the Diary Room and asked me questions about Rachel's eviction, Brendon's HoH win, my third stint as a Have-Not, and my nomination. I always have a hard time falling asleep but it can take me hours to drift off when I am anxious. My mind raced last night. The week's events fell before my mind's eye like Tetris bricks. Maybe I was too hard on Rachel. If I am evicted this week, I will not earn $20,000 for my saboteur duties. And I will be alone in the jury house with Rachel. I wonder what the Veto competition will be. If I win Veto, Matt will likely be the replacement nominee and I do not want to be responsible for him leaving. This obsessive pattern of thinking went on for hours. I was nearly asleep when production called me to the DR at 2 a.m. After five weeks in the house, I finally lost my cool with producers. "Are you trying to sabotage me," I asked. "Tomorrow is the Veto competition and you keep demanding I come into the Diary Room. I need sleep!"

Anxiety has killed my appetite. No slop for me this morning. My stomach is in a surgeon's knot when I walk to the backyard and catch my first glimpse of the Veto competition. Six people will compete in today's contest. Each of us starts at one end of a balance beam, where a basket is filled with puzzle pieces. Each player selects one puzzle piece, walks it across the beam, and then hops onto a mechanized circle that spins. Once we successfully place one piece of puzzle into its frame, we walk back across the balance beam and repeat the process. If a player falls off the apparatus, he or she is eliminated from the competition. The first person to complete his or her puzzle wins the coveted Power of Veto.

Anxiety transforms into tunnel vision as I carefully make my way from one side of the beam to the next and make quick work of the puzzle. Brendon is on the beam directly to my left. I notice him studying my jigsaw, as he tries to figure out a pattern that might help him catch up to me. Everyone else is far behind the two of us; and Brendon is not even midway done with the brainteaser when I slip the final piece into place, walk back to the starting side of the beam, and press a button that signifies I am done. Yes! Forty-eight hours of misery have given way to blissful triumph. I have taken down my bully! Adrenaline pulsates through my body as the PoV medallion is placed around my neck.

Two hours after my victory, Matt, Enzo, and I relax in a room dubbed "The Taj" because its luxe Persian design is reminiscent of the Taj Mahal. We are midway through rehashing the Veto competition when the front doorbell rings. As if cued by a script, we each shoot a bewildered look at one another. The front doorbell rarely rings; and, when it does, good fortune usually rains upon the house. One season, pop superstar Sheryl Crow visited the house and performed a concert. Last year, actor Jeremy Piven knocked on the front door and spent the day with the houseguests. Could today get any better? I spin on my heels and race to the door. My heart plummets into my stomach after I answer the door and Rachel stomps past me. "Ha, ha, ha, I'm back, bitches! And now you guys have to deal with me for 24 hours. Are you shocked, Ragan," Rachel teases.

"I'm not shocked, Rachel. I'm disgusted," I shoot back.

"Why don't you get us a drink, Ra-tress?" A group of producers laughing booms over the speakers. This is the first time in five weeks I have heard producers react to a house event. They clearly forgot to turn off their microphones. Their raucous laughter is immediately cut from the speakers with an electric "pop," indicating they quickly muted the production mic.

"Do you have to be the biggest bitch because you're gay?"

CBS's edited footage

> The double beat of a drum tears through the moment.
> Cut to Matt raising both his eyebrows.
> Cut to Hayden shifting his expressionless face to Rachel.
> A high-pitch cymbal reverberates.
> Cut to Lane standing near-frozen with his mouth agape.
> Cut to Kathy with her right hand covering the lower half of her mouth.
> Cut to Britney seated behind me with her lips stuck in an "O" shape.

"No, Rachel, I'm not a big bitch because I'm gay. I'm a big bitch because you're an absolute monster. Count your friends in the house. Done already?"

"I'll make every minute of the [next] 24 hours miserable for you, Ragan."

"Back at ya," I reply.

"Good. Please do. Please try."

> *In the next segment, Rachel learns I am a Have-Not for the week.*
> *She comes outside with a package of unbaked cookies.*

"Hey, Ragan, I'm going to make some really big, soft, gooey cookies. Do you want some?"

I sit on a workout bench taking a rest between bench-press sets. I look up at Rachel as she approaches me. "Rachel, you don't intimidate me. You repulse me. You're about as classy as your nasty hair extensions."

"I travel around the world—" she boasts.

I raise the pitch of my voice, stand up, and imitate Rachel. I jokingly say, "I travel around the world and I go to Vegas. And I lie about $20,000 bottles of wine."

"What did I lie about?"

"*Everything* about you is a lie. Your boobs are a lie. Your face is a lie. The only thing honest about you is the pimple on your chin." I no longer feel in control of my words and actions. I am in a zone I have only ever experienced when performing literature and going to a place where I am no longer playing at a character, I have become the drama I recite. Anxiety furiously thumps through my veins. I am stuck somewhere between fight and flight. I stand up, tell her to leave me alone, and make my way inside. I stare Rachel down as I march past her. Never one to back down from a fight—even one she is losing—Rachel trails behind me.

"Why don't you try to insult me a little more, Ragan," she asks.

"Why do you try to insult me? Why don't you talk about me being gay? And me being a bitch."

"Because I love gay people and you suck at it."

"Yes, you clearly love gay people. One day you will realize that the attention that you want is not from negative behavior but by treating people with decency and respect. If you think you're going to go through life running over people and treating them like you've treated everybody in this house, you have another thing coming. You will get what is coming to you. Take it as a tip and learn from it," I spit. I slam the sliding door shut behind me. Rachel stands in dead silence for a full minute and a half. Other than biting her lips, she appears dizzy and paralyzed. None of the other houseguests in the backyard utter a word. Kathy smokes a cigarette and refuses to make eye contact. Britney hits balls on the pool table. Rachel eventually moves one foot in front of the next, opens the door, and steps back inside.

Being here

My fight with Rachel was not scripted but it was intricately orchestrated by production. A few days before Rachel's eviction, producers called me into the DR and pitched my final act of sabotage for the week. They proposed that I glue the front door shut. Sealing the front door meant Rachel would not be able to leave once she was evicted. She would technically be out of the game but would have to stay in the house for a few days. Producers enticed me with the prospect of humiliating Rachel. I quickly realized that the stunt would be more torturous for me and my allies than Rachel and Brendon. Production's request became more intense when they included co-executive producer Rich Meehan in on our conversation. Rich promised that the prank would put me in the *Big Brother* history books. After a few separate, pressure-filled Diary Room sessions, producers finally gave up. I apologized to them for declining their proposal. Their reaction was surprisingly calm given how much they previously insisted I perform the act of sabotage.

Rachel's return to the house emerged after Brendon won Head of Household and producers presented him with Pandora's Box. The houseguest who opens Pandora's Box releases something good and something bad in the house. In this case, Brendon got to visit a vacation resort, where he was wined, dined, and massaged. We realized Brendon was missing after Rachel arrived. As I pointed out to Rachel during our argument, she was only in the house for 24 hours because her boyfriend obviously opened a Pandora's Box and unleashed "something horrible" on the rest of us. Rachel returning to the house two days after her eviction taught me that *Big Brother*'s producers have multiple ways to manufacture outcomes they believe will heighten the show's drama.

Several months after *Big Brother 12*'s finale, a story producer for the show approached me at a gay bar in West Hollywood and introduced himself. "That fight with Rachel was amazing," he exclaimed. He told me that he played a significant role in editing the scene for CBS's broadcast. "Originally, they didn't edit in the reaction shots. Rachel said something about you being a bitch because you're gay, and then they immediately cut to your response. I was like, 'Oh, no. We should let that moment sink in.' We need shots of everyone reacting to her anti-gay statements." I tried to imagine the scene without Matt's raised eyebrows, Lane's openmouthed stare, and Britney's look of disgust. Their silent reactions and production's use of dramatic music punctuate Rachel's homophobic insult. The gay producer's intervention ensured that homophobia would be treated as a critical component of our dispute. Our disagreement was not like others in the house. My sexuality—a sexuality that was rendered impotent by the peri-performative constraints of the program—had come under attack.

A third and final signification of reading helps theorize the role gay reality show producers and participants play in the production of LGBTQ performativity. *Queer reading*, also known as "queering," references a specific method of textual engagement, where critics explore the queer potential of a text. Queering characterizes a form of cultural spectatorship that critiques heteronormativity and celebrates non-normative expressions of gender and sexuality. The practice calls attention to and critiques hetero-"textual essentialism," or the tendency to assume heterosexual themes, characters, and behaviors even when heterosexuality is not explicitly stated.[88] Queer readings demonstrate how LGBTQ people are culturally positioned to articulate unique interpretations of an event, behavior, or space. Queering "involves a commitment to 'queer world-making,' or the presentation of alternate worldviews that run alongside, rather than replace, master narratives."[89] Casting sexual minorities on reality TV programs and hiring sexual minorities as producers enable gay and lesbian people to share their insights and critiques of heteronormativity, or the belief that heterosexuality is the only viable option. The gay producer's insistence that story editors pause after Rachel's insult and cut to other houseguests' looks of discomfort demonstrate his queer reading of the argument. Had he not intervened, the scene might have amounted to little more than an overdramatic gay flamer hurling insults at a woman.

Narrating in a Scholarly "Diary Room"

Being there. September 2, 2010

Julie Chen announces that I am the ninth player eliminated from the game. I hug the remaining four houseguests, and eagerly make my way out of the house and into a cheering crowd. Sweat drenches my armpits as I approach Julie. I offer her my right hand, which she rejects in favor of a tight, warm hug. We sit down on her post-eviction couch.

"Ragan," Julie says with a warm smile, "we saw a very emotional side to you in the house. What did you learn about yourself?"

"I learned that I'm an emotional person, but being emotional isn't weak. I was able to go up against athletes and strong-minded people, and really hold my own. I learned that, in my darkest hours, I dig deep for resources and do what I have to do to get to the next day."

Being here

Throughout *Big Brother*, I found myself ensnared in a web of gay representation. The more I resisted the constraints, assumptions, and projections that preceded and shaped my ability to perform sexual identity, the more the web trapped me. These conventions, or tropes, "work to confine homosexuality within its paradoxical position in dominant heteronormative discourses; homosexuality can only be represented through heterosexist categories and language, while at the same time it is marked as a deviation from the norm."[90]

My performance of gay identity on *Big Brother* represents a "burden of synecdoche,"[91] or an expectation for one member of a marginalized group to "properly" represent the implicated community's genius, talent, and best qualities. This burden exemplifies what Eve Sedgwick characterizes as minoritizing logic. Sedgwick uses "minoritizing" and "universalizing" as an "alternative (though not an equivalent to) essentialist and constructivist."[92] The terms underscore how essentialist rhetoric uniquely complicates the lives of gay people. Burden of synecdoche is minoritizing logic in two key ways. First, burden of synecdoche is a paradox, because no gay man or lesbian can meet the conflicting standards and impossible demands that comprise exemplary representation of a racially, ethnically, and socioeconomically diverse community.

Second, the burden is a form of tokenizing logic. Take, for example, the following statement made by my housemate Hayden: "Ragan, you are an awesome representative of the gay community." While I certainly appreciate Hayden's sentiment, I question its rhetorical implications. I, unlike Hayden, must serve as an exemplar of a historically marginalized group and play a game known for lying and backstabbing. Hayden's statement also indirectly implies that the gay community lacks awesome representatives. Keep in mind, my self-presentation in the house was relatively mundane. If eating, sleeping, showering, and competing are the sole criteria for performing the role of "awesome representative of the gay community," I wonder what Hayden and perhaps many viewers may think is a more typical representation of gay men.

Gays on primetime TV alter many of the misrepresentative myths upon which homophobia exerts itself. More than any other time in TV history, gay people have been present in primetime and exert control over how their characters/selves are portrayed. Conversely, the burden of synecdoche paradox partially shapes how these characters are read. When viewers tokenize gay characters, they expect for them to be exemplary representatives of their communities; and, if they fail to exemplify greatness, their failures and character flaws—no matter how mundane—are used to justify bigoted attitudes and narratize the assumed worst elements of a gay person's character.

Theories of narratization may help media scholars explicate performative readings audience members create when they visit fan forums and provide commentary of shows they watch. Typically, performativity is discussed as a method of enactment. This project situates performativity in phenomenological terms and emphasizes unique ways that audience members play a significant role in constructing characters and narratives they view on television. I describe this phenomenon as a "performative reading" to highlight how reception is also an act of production. Theories of narratization situate audience members as co-producers of mediated events, which in turn challenges the idea that media texts simply "reflect their relationship to one another more than they reflect reality."[93] Scholars who suggest that reality TV producers "should not claim to reflect reality"[94] because "by definition, they mediate"[95] may fail to recognize the extent to which all forms of narrative—both on and off TV—are mediated. Bifurcating reality and television, while privileging "reality" as more authentic, misses the point of critical theory. The interpretive model proposed in this book provides a more nuanced way to articulate how performative enactments and performative readings of identity undergo a complex process of phenomenological mediation.

86 Fagan: Awesome Representative

Notes

1 Walter Fisher, "Narration as a Human Communication Paradigm," *Communication Monographs* 51, no. 1 (2984): 1–21.
2 John M. Allison, "Narrative and Time: A Phenomenological Reconsideration," *Text and Performance Quarterly* 14, no 2 (1994): 108–25.
3 Julian Jaynes, *The Origin of Consciousness in the Breakdown of the Bicameral Mind* (Boston, MA: Mariner, 1990), 63–4.
4 Edumund Husserl, *The Phenomenology of Internal Time Consciousness*, trans. James Churchill (Bloomington: Indiana University Press, 1964), 111.
5 Ibid., 120–1.
6 Bonnie J. Dow, "Ellen, Television, and the Politics of Gay and Lesbian Visibility," *Critical Studies in Media Communication* 18, no. 2 (2001): 129.
7 Kathleen Battles and Wendy Hilton-Morrow, "Gay Characters in Conventional Spaces: Will and Grace and the Situation Comedy Genre," *Critical Studies in Media Communication* 19, no. 1 (2002): 94.
8 Helene A. Shugart, "Reinventing Privilege: The New (Gay) Man in Contemporary Popular Media," *Critical Studies in Media Communication* 20, no. 1 (2003): 70.
9 Guillermo Avila-Saavedra, "Nothing Queer about Queer Television: Televised Construction of Gay Masculinities," *Media, Culture, and Society* 31, no. 1 (2009): 8.
10 Alexander Doty, *Flaming Classics: Queering the Film Canon* (New York, NY: Routledge, 2000), 5.
11 Michaela D. Meyer and John M. Kelley, "Queering the Eye? The Politics of Gay White Men and Gender (In)visibility," *Feminist Media Studies* 4, no. 3 (2004): 214–17.
12 Suzanna D. Walters, *All the Rage: The Story of Gay Visibility in America* (Chicago, IL: University of Chicago Press, 2003).
13 Jay Clarkson, "Contesting Masculinity's Makeover: Queer Eye, Consumer Masculinity, and 'Straight-Acting' Gays," *Journal of Communication Inquiry* 29, no. 3 (2005): 235–55.
14 Diane Raymond, "Popular Culture and Queer Representation: A Critical Perspective," *Gender, Race, and Class in Media: A Text Reader*, ed. Gail Dines and Jean M. Humez (Thousand Oaks, CA: Sage, 2003), 107.
15 Stephen Tropiano, *The Prime Time Closet: A History of Gays and Lesbians on TV* (New York, NY: Applause Theatre and Cinema, 2002).
16 A.J. Jacobs, "When Gay Men Happen to Straight Wome," *Entertainment Weekly*, October 23, 1998, 20; Helene A. Shugart, "Reinventing Privilege."
17 George Gerbner and Larry Gross. "Living with Television: The Violence Profile," *Journal of Communication* 26, no. 2 (1976): 172–94.
18 Fred Fejes and Kevin Petrich, "Invisibility, Homophobia and Heterosexism: Lesbians, Gays and the Media," *Critical Studies in Mass Communication* 10, no. 4 (1993): 409.
19 Robert A. Brookey Robert Westerfelhaus, "Pistols and Petticoats, Piety and Purity: To Wong Foo, the Queering of the American Monomyth, and the Marginalizing Discourse of Deification," *Critical Studies in Media Communication* 18, no. 2 (2001): 151.
20 Robin Boylorn, "As Seen on TV: An Autoethnographic Reflection on Race and Reality Television," *Critical Studies in Media Communication* 25, no. 4 (2008): 413–33.
21 John Fiske, *Television Culture* (New York, NY: Routledge, 1987).
22 Robert Alan Brookey and Robert Westerfelhaus, "Hiding Homoeroticism in Plain View: The Fight Club DVD as Digital Closet," *Critical Studies in Media Communication* 19, no. 1 (2002): 22.
23 Rachel E. Dubrofsky, "Fallen Women in Reality TV: A Pornography of Emotion," *Feminist Media Studies* 29, no. 3 (2009): 353.
24 Mike Donaldson, "What Is Hegemonic Masculinity?" *Theory and Society* 22, no. 5 (1993): 643–57.

25 Shinsuke Eguchi, "Negotiating Hegemonic Masculinity: The Rhetorical Strategy of 'Straight-Acting' Among Gay Men," *Journal of Intercultural Communication Research* 38, no. 3 (2009): 193–209.

26 Larry P. Gross, *Up from Invisibility: Lesbians, Gay Men and the Media in America* (New York, NY: Columbia University Press, 2001); Diane Raymond, "Popular Culture and Queer Representation."

27 Lauren Dundes and Alan Dundes, "Young Hero Simba Defeats Old Villain Scar: Oedipus Wrecks the Lyin' King," *The Social Science Journal* 43, no. 3 (2006): 479–85.

28 Alexander Doty, *Flaming Classics*.

29 Rodger Streitmatter, *From 'Perverts' to 'Fab Five': The Media's Changing Depiction of Gay Men and Lesbians* (New York, NY: Taylor and Francis, 2009).

30 Bonnie Dow, "Ellen, Television, and the Politics of Gay and Lesbian Visibility," 129.

31 Fred Fejes and Kevin Petrich, "Invisibility, Homophobia and Heterosexism: Lesbians, Gays and the Media," 401.

32 Ibid., 398.

33 Victoria79, "Fagan: 'Awesome' Representative of the Gay Community," *Survivor Sucks*, August 25, 2010, http://SurvivorSucks.com/topic/71737/Fagan-Awesome-Representative-Gay- Community-s-made-proud?page=55.

34 Garblue, "Fagan: 'Awesome' Representative of the Gay Community," *Survivor Sucks*, August 26, 2010, http://SurvivorSucks.com/topic/71737/Fagan-Awesome-Representative-Gay-Commu-nity-s-made-proud?page=58.

35 BBjXavier, "Fagan: 'Awesome' Representative of the Gay Community," *Survivor Sucks*, August 25, 2010, http://SurvivorSucks.com/topic/71737/Fagan-Awesome-Representative-Gay-Community-s-made-proud?page=55.

36 Buttsecks, "Fagan: 'Awesome' Representative of the Gay Community," *Survivor Sucks*, August 26, 2010, http://SurvivorSucks.com/topic/71737/Fagan-Awesome-Representative-Gay-Community-s-made-proud?page=57.

37 FLgirl, "Fagan: 'Awesome' Representative of the Gay Community," *Survivor Sucks*, August 29, 2010, http://SurvivorSucks.com/topic/71737/Fagan-Awesome-Representative-Gay-Community-s-made-proud?page=60.

38 Fisherman39, "Fagan: 'Awesome' Representative of the Gay Community," *Survivor Sucks*, August 26, 2010, http://SurvivorSucks.com/topic/71737/Fagan-Awesome-Representative-Gay-Community-s-made--proud?page=56.

39 Xrealitydotnet, "Fagan: 'Awesome' Representative of the Gay Community," *Survivor Sucks*, August 26, 2010, http://SurvivorSucks.com/topic/71737/Fagan-Awesome-Representative-Gay-Community-s-made-proud?page=56.

40 Julian Jaynes, *The Origin of Consciousness in the Breakdown of the Bicameral Mind*, 64.

41 ArtMaggot, "How to Tame a Stallion," *Survivor Sucks*, July 7, 2010, http://Survivor Sucks.yuku.com/topic/71680/BB12-OFFICIAL-Photochop-Thread?page=10.

42 ArtMaggot, "The Ass Whisperer," *Survivor Sucks*, July 3, 2010, http://SurvivorSucks. yuku.com/topic/71680/BB12-OFFICIAL-Photochop-Thread?page=5.

43 Kathleen Battles and Wendy Hilton-Morrow, "Gay Characters in Conventional Spaces," 99.

44 Joanne R. Gilbert, *Performing Marginality: Humor, Gender, and Cultural Critique* (Detroit, MI: Wayne State University Press, 2004), 12.

45 Diane Raymond, "Popular Culture and Queer Representation," 108.

46 EgregiousPhilbin, "Single White Shemale," August 19, 2010, http://SurvivorSucks. yuku.com/topic/71680/BB12-OFFICIAL-Photochop-Thread?page=46.

47 George Chauncey, *Gay New York: Gender, Urban Culture, and the Making of the Gay Male World* (New York, NY: Basic Books, 1994), 15.

48 Joseph Goodwin, *More Man Than You'll Ever Be: Gay Folklore and Acculturation in Middle America* (Bloomington, IN: Indiana University Press, 1989), 61.

49 Christopher Pullen, *The Household, the Basement and the Real World, Understanding Reality Television*, ed. Su Holmes and Deborah Jermyn (New York, NY: Routledge, 2004), 213.

50 Ronald J. Testa, Bill N. Kinder, and Gail Ironson, "Heterosexual Bias in the Perception of Loving Relationships of Gay Males and Lesbians," *The Journal of Sex Research* 23, no. 2 (1987): 163–72.

51 Archimedes, "Flame On," *Survivor Sucks*, July 18, 2010, http://survivorsucks.yuku.com/topic/71680/BB12-OFFICIAL-Photochop-Thread?page=22.

52 OttoJr, "'Awesome' Representative of the Gay Community," *Survivor Sucks*, June 30, 2010, http://survivorsucks.yuku.com/search/topic/topic/71737.

53 WylDog, "'Awesome' Representative of the Gay Community," *Survivor Sucks*, June 30, 2010, http://survivorsucks.yuku.com/search/topic/topic/71737.

54 Fagan, "'Awesome' Representative of the Gay Community," *Survivor Sucks*, June 30, 2017, http://survivorsucks.yuku.com/search/topic/topic/71737.

55 Earthdog, "Will & Grace," *Survivor Sucks*, July 2, 2010, http://survivorsucks.yuku.com/topic/71680/BB12-OFFICIAL-Photochop-Thread?page=4#.WTdOrcaZOu4.

56 Karen1407, "Howie Splashed Me with Water. I Quit! Marcy Hate," *Survivor Sucks*, July 15, 2006, http://survivorsucks.yuku.com/search/topic/topic/5211.

57 CuauhtemocCosby, "Howie Splashed Me with Water. I Quit! Marcy Hate," *Survivor Sucks*, August 4, 2006, http://survivorsucks.yuku.com/search/topic/topic/5211.

58 Tritonsrod, "Dustin Hate!" *Survivor Sucks*, July 26, 2007, http://survivorsucks.yuku.com/search/topic/topic/4868.

59 Nomiiiii, "Dustin Hate!" *Survivor Sucks*, July 17, 2007, http://survivorsucks.yuku.com/search/topic/topic/4868.

60 JesusOfNajareth, "Dustin Hate!" *Survivor Sucks*, August 16, 2007, http://survivorsucks.yuku.com/search/topic/topic/4868.

61 DaveSoGay, "Little Piggy Is Out: By Josh! Good Plan!" *Survivor Sucks*, March 3, 2008, http://survivorsucks.yuku.com/search/topic/topic/27130.

62 ScruffyGuy, "Little Piggy Is Out. By Josh! Good Plan!" *Survivor Sucks*, March 5, 2008, http://survivorsucks.yuku.com/search/topic/topic/27130.

63 Daguerreo, "Kevin, You Suck! Get Out of Cuntalies Ass!" *Survivor Sucks*, September 2, 2009, http://survivorsucks.yuku.com/search/topic/topic/53838.

64 LoungeAct, "Kevin, You Suck! Get Out of Cuntalies Ass!" *Survivor Sucks*, September 8, 2009, http://survivorsucks.yuku.com/search/topic/topic/53838.

65 Buttsecks, "Wil—Manliest Voice Since Jay Byars," *Survivor Sucks*, July 4, 2012, http://survivorsucks.yuku.com/topic/96939/Wil-Manliest-Voice-since-Jay-Byars?page=3.

66 SurvivorNinja, "Wil—ManliestVoice Since Jay Byars," *Survivor Sucks*, July 4, 2012, http://survivorsucks.yuku.com/topic/96939/Wil-Manliest-Voice-since-Jay-Byars?page=3.

67 Riff, "Andy Love Thread! Inner Bitches!!! Best Player Since Dan!" *Survivor Sucks*, August 31, 2013, http://survivorsucks.yuku.com/search/topic/topic/113339.

68 Riff, "Frankie Is the Literal Worst," *Survivor Sucks*, August 10, 2014, http://survivorsucks.yuku.com/search/topic/topic/121776.

69 SardonicallyIrrelevant, "Josea Flores—His Is Not Risen," *Survivor Sucks*, June 24, 2016, http://survivorsucks.yuku.com/search/topic/topic/128974.

70 Moovivor, "Josea Flores—His Is Not Risen," *Survivor Sucks*, June 23, 2016, http://survivorsucks.yuku.com/search/topic/topic/128974.

71 Judith Butler, *Bodies that Matter: On the Discursive Limits of 'Sex'*, 2.

72 Ibid., 3.

73 Adi Kuntsman, "Belonging through Violence: Flaming, Erasure, and Performativity in Queer Migrant Community," *Queer Online: Media Technology and Sexuality*, ed. Kate O'Riordan and David J. Phillips (New York, NY: Peter Lang, 2007), 104.

74 Rhea Ashley Hoskin, "Femme Theory: Refocusing the Intersectional Lens," *Atlantis: Critical Studies in Gender, Culture, and Social Justice* 38, no. 1 (2017): 102.

75 Ibid.
76 UNCDavid, "These Comps Are Totally Rigged for Midgets and Gays," *Survivor Sucks*, August 9, 2010, http://survivorsucks.yuku.com/topic/71680/BB12-OFFICIAL-Photochop-Thread?page=42#.WTdUgMaZOu4.
77 Earthdog, "Sunset Boulevard," *Survivor Sucks*, August 26, 2010, http://survivorsucks.yuku.com/topic/71680/BB12-OFFICIAL-Photochop-Thread?page=50.
78 KudrowFan, "'Awesome' Representative of the Gay Community," *Survivor Sucks*, June 30, 2010, http://survivorsucks.yuku.com/search/topic/topic/71737.
79 Xanster82, "'Awesome' Representative of the Gay Community," *Survivor Sucks*, June 30, 2010, http://survivorsucks.yuku.com/search/topic/topic/71737.
80 Michel Foucault, *The History of Sexuality, Volume 1: An Introduction*, trans. Robert Hurley (New York, NY: Vintage, 1978), 18.
81 Ibid., 35.
82 Gilbert Herdt, *Same Sex, Different Cultures: Exploring Gay and Lesbian Lives* (Boulder, CO: Westview Press, 1997), 33.
83 EgregiousPhilbin, *Survivor Sucks*, July 16, 2010, http://survivorsucks.yuku.com/search/topic/topic/71680.
84 Artmaggot, *Survivor Sucks*, July 17, 2010, http://survivorsucks.yuku.com/topic/71680/BB12-OFFICIAL-Photochop-Thread?page=21#.WT8348aZOu4.
85 Peter M. Nardi and Nancy E. Stoller, "'Fruits,' 'Fags,' and 'Dykes': The Portrayal of Gay/Lesbian Identity in 'Nance' Jokes of the '50s and '60s'," *Journal of Homosexuality* 55, no. 3 (2008): 408.
86 Ibid.
87 Jarett Wieselman, "Rachel Got Owned Last Night on Big Brother," *New York Post*, August 19, 2010.
88 Alexander Doty, *Flaming Classics: Queering the Film Canon* (New York, NY: Routledge, 2000), 3.
89 Ragan Fox, "'Homo'-work: Queering Academic Communication and Communicating Queer in Academia," *Text and Performance Quarterly* 33, no. 1 (2013): 62.
90 Kathleen Battles and Wendy Hilton-Morrow, "Gay Characters in Conventional Spaces," 101–2.
91 Jacqueline Taylor, "On Being an Exemplary Lesbian: My Life as a Role Model," *Text and Performance Quarterly* 20, no. 1 (2000): 72.
92 Eve Kosofsky Sedgwick, *Epistemology of the Closet* (Berkeley: University of California Press, 1990), 40.
93 Katrina Bell-Jordan, "Black. White. and a Survivor of the Real World: Constructions of Race on Reality TV," *Critical Studies in Media Communication*, 25, no. 4 (2008): 369.
94 Ibid.
95 Laura Grindstaff, *The Money Shot: Trash, Class, and the Making of TV Talk Shows* (Chicago: University of Chicago Press, 2002), 249.

Interlude

Being there

Six months after *Big Brother 12*'s finale, my favorite person from production, Sheila, invited me to lunch. *Big Brother*'s production team is never direct when they want something from a houseguest. Nearly a year prior to our lunch date, Sheila cloaked my casting reveal in a request for B-roll footage of me teaching. These men and women have produced 12 seasons of a show known for its participants' machinations and maneuvering. People like Sheila know how to exploit the exploiters.

I arrive at lunch aware that 1) CBS wants something from me, and 2) the network sent Sheila to either collect information from me or assess my interest in returning to the program. After small talk, Sheila takes a gulp of her iced tea and asks about my relationship with Rachel. Are we getting along?

"Yes. After the season ended, I felt bad for the way fans treated her. We reconnected and have hung out a few times," I tell her. "She asked me to be in her wedding." Sheila arches her right eyebrow and chuckles.

A few weeks after my lunch date with Sheila, Rachel confesses that production has also approached her and asked a series of mysterious questions. Trained by production to keep a locked lip, neither of us will come right out and say what we think: the network wants one or both of us to return. Rachel and I take turns metaphorically winking at one another and making sarcastic statements like, "It's so nice that production is keeping in touch with us. I'm sure they have no ulterior motive. It's funny how we're the only two people they've contacted since the finale."

92 Interlude

Months go by and I do not hear back from producers. One night in June, Brendon and Rachel invite me over to their apartment in Westwood and divulge that they have been invited back for Season 13. Suddenly, my lunch with Sheila makes sense. Had Rachel and I still been quarreling, they would have probably asked us back individually and then made us play as a duo. "They're bringing back pairs," I predict. "They wouldn't just bring back one couple. It's either an all-stars season where everyone returning will be in some sort of duo, or they'll make it a mix of new players and returning twosomes." I tell Rachel and Brendon that producers will likely ask Season 11 sweethearts Jeff and Jordan to return. Like Brendon and Rachel, Jeff and Jordan met on the show and fell in love. "If Jeff and Jordan are in the house, make sure you win the first HoH competition and immediately form an alliance with them. America loves Jeff and Jordan and so does production. If you group up with them, you'll benefit from producers working magic to keep them in the game."

Being here

Sure enough, Season 13's twist centered around three returning duos, including Season 11's Jeff and Jordan, the couple America loves; Season 12's Brendon and Rachel, the couple America loves to hate; and Season 8's Dick and Danielle, a father and daughter who hate one another.

Season 13 represented a liminal, or transitional, period for me in relation to *Big Brother*. I was neither a typical viewer nor a member of the season's cast. I was, however, peripherally involved with the program in several ways. First, Superpass, the company that ran *Big Brother*'s 24-hour Internet live feed, hired me to host a weekly call-in show for their viewers. Audience members calling into my program often discussed controversies and activities that had not yet been broadcast on CBS's edit of *Big Brother*. Their up-to-the-minute commentary meant I had to watch *Big Brother*'s Internet feed, otherwise I would have little to offer to the dialogue.

Next, I am pals with three of the returning players: Brendon, Rachel, and Danielle. Watching a friend compete on a reality program bolsters the investment one makes while viewing. The year after my stint on *Big Brother*, friends and family members explained how difficult it was to see people double-cross me in the house and so-called super fans write mean-spirited comments about me in message forums. My relationships with Brendon, Rachel, and Danielle placed me in the frustrating position occupied by my loved ones when they watched me compete.

Finally, CBS visited my home and filmed a segment where I discussed Rachel's gameplay. CBS featured my commentary on the show's network broadcast. A *Big Brother* producer initially wanted me to film the package at no cost. "Ragan, you're worth more than free," my friend and *Big Brother 12* co-star Britney reminded me. After rigorous negotiations, CBS agreed to pay me a mere $200 for my labor. The low economic value the network placed on my contribution to Season 13 illustrates one of the ways that *Big Brother* functions as a "theatre of neoliberalism," where the play and prizes characteristic of a gameshow cloak CBS's "regime of economic production."[1] From the network's perspective, I should feel honored to be invited back and returning to television is adequate payment.

A magical thing happened the year after my stint on *Big Brother 12*. I began to see the series as labor instead of recreation. *Big Brother* was no longer my favorite television show; it was work. I could now see and hear things in the CBS broadcast that were once invisible to me, such as producer prompts that would likely generate specific outcomes in the house and enhance the program's drama. My experiences on Season 12 helped me pinpoint the program's contrivances. One time, for example, I entered the Diary Room to vent about Brendon and Rachel making out in the Have-Not room while I was trying to sleep. A producer repeatedly urged me to air my frustrations with the notoriously reactive couple.

I became a more culturally reflexive viewer when I watched *Big Brother 13*. Reading stereotype-laden fan criticism about my self-representation encouraged me to be more critical of the ways in which viewers comment on other *Big Brother* houseguests from historically marginalized groups. In the following chapter, I investigate fan commentary about race and gender on *Big Brother* and consider how the series' producers address in-house racism in CBS's broadcast.

Note

1 Nick Couldry, "Reality TV, or the Secret Theater of Neoliberalism," *Review of Education, Pedagogy, and Cultural Studies* 30, no. 3 (2008): 3–13.

4

PERFORMATIVELY SPECTATING HOUSEGUESTS OF COLOR

In 2012, social media outlets erupted after the *New York Times* labeled even-keeled First Lady Michelle Obama an "angry Black woman." Nigerian novelist Chimamanda Ngozi Adichie writes, "Because she said what she thought, and because she smiled only when she felt like smiling, and not constantly and vacuously, America's cheapest caricature was cast on her: the Angry Black Woman."[1]

Reductive, stereotype-focused readings of Black men and women are just as insidious on reality television, where people of color cannot escape the contradictory rules that govern the interpretation of their identities. Producers and viewers often expect people of color to fit into racial archetypes. The moment a Black woman raises her voice in the *Big Brother* house, she becomes the proof of the truth of the angry, Black woman stereotype. Her anger authenticates her Blackness and emotionality/femininity and lends credence to *Big Brother*'s purported reality. Patricia Hill Collins argues that "gender-specific images of Black bitches and bad mothers [have] flourished in this [mediated] climate."[2]

Some *Big Brother* fans, for instance, proved particularly brutal in their reading of *Big Brother 10*'s sole Black female contestant, Libra. Many *Survivor* Sucks participants suggested that Libra epitomizes the "mad black woman" (see Figure 4.1). Viewers also criticized the Rice University graduate for leaving her two small children at home so she could be a contestant on the program. Fans referred to Libra's children as "abandoned babies"[3] and suggested, "Maybe she hates her kids."[4] In my decade of watching *Big Brother*, Libra is the only parent I have seen fans take to task for misguided perceptions of child abandonment. SurvivorArctic's impression that Libra "hates her kids" demonstrates how the angry Black woman stereotype may be linked to images of bad Black mothers. The viewer intimates that Libra's ability to leave her children for a single summer is connected to hatred, or an alleged innate anger that presumably resides in all women of color.

96 Houseguests of Color

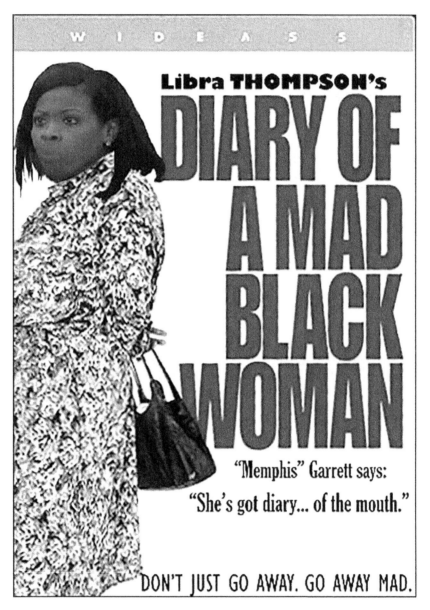

FIGURE 4.1   Photosphopped image of *Big Brother* 10's Libra[5]

The angry Black woman trope is one of *Big Brother*'s principle authenticating devices, or "authenticating acts." Authenticating acts are referential behaviors actors and audience members believe "reveal or produce the 'true' self."[6] Television programs like *Big Brother* validate through a reality-constituting, circular logic whereby 1) authenticating acts like Black rage and gay tears prove that character exploits are grounded in so-called reality, and 2) the genre's "reality" classification substantiates stereotypes associated with participants from historically marginalized communities.

White, cisgender, heterosexual men do not have to performatively validate their whiteness and heterosexuality in the same manner as a gay player or contestant of color because their pigment and sexual inclinations are often framed as the absence of race and sexuality. This manufactured void of race and sexuality ironically disguises the various ways in which whiteness and heterosexuality are exceedingly present in the United States. Fans of *Big Brother*, for instance, never identify White, straight houseguests as "good" or "bad" representatives of their communities in the same manner sexual minorities and people of color are treated as emblematic of their communities. Not only do White, heterosexual men not shoulder the same burden of representation as queer houseguests and contestants of color, but they are praised when they counter performative expectations. A White, heterosexual contestant's anger may be framed as a culturally valid expression of masculinity because aggression is culturally coded as a male performative, or a proper means for White men to perform their gender.[7] Ironically, the same man's tears might be interpreted as brave insofar as he subverts social pressure to contain his emotions.

In this chapter, I investigate the rhetorical construction of race and racism on seasons 11, 13, and 15 of *Big Brother*. I focus on these seasons for a few reasons. *Big Brother 11*, *13*, and *15* feature casts more racially diverse than other seasons. *Big Brother 11*'s 14 houseguests include an Argentinian and Black woman named Natalie, a Lebanese man named Russell, a Latina named Lydia, a Black woman named Chima, and a Japanese and Black man named Kevin. A Black man named Lawon, a Black woman named Kalia, a Black man named Keith, a Latino man named Brendon, and a Filipino man named Dominic comprise five of fourteen positions in *Big Brother 13*'s cast. *Big Brother 15*'s contestants include a Black woman named Candice, a Black man named Howard, and a Korean woman named Helen. Season 15 is more notable for racist controversies than its diverse cast. I include *Big Brother 15* in my analysis because multiple forms of performative spectatorship likely prompted the show's producers to directly address racism in the *Big Brother* house. Despite boasting racially and ethnically diverse casts for more than a decade, Season 15 marked the first time *Big Brother*'s production team made racism a salient topic in its CBS broadcast.

Racist Tropes of Representation

In her linguistic critique of racism on reality television, Rebecca Pardo notes that because, "It is no longer commonly acceptable to make explicit comments disparaging racial minorities because of alleged biological deficiencies; racism is now more often expressed in terms of cultural stereotypes."[8] Mark Orbe contends that many reality television shows reinforce racist caricatures that dehumanize and marginalize people of color.[9] Critical media researchers have focused on how race is rhetorically constructed by producers of and contestants on *The Bachelor* and *Flavor of Love*,[10] presented as anti-essentialist in its depiction of Black fatherhood on *Run's House* and *Snoop Dogg's Father Hood*,[11] a rhetorical device used to normalize White surveillance and perpetuate myths of Black criminality on *Cops* and *World's Wildest Police Videos*,[12] and reductively depicted through the use of the angry Black woman trope on MTV's *Road Rules*.[13]

Surprisingly, few media studies scholars investigate how audience members rely on racist archetypes when spectating a reality show. I characterize this dearth of research as "surprising" because poststructural characteristics (e.g., the intentional fallacy) celebrated in critical-cultural scholarship focus on what audience members *do* with texts they consume. In other words, how might spectators use stereotypes to interpret people of color, regardless of how those characters are depicted on a program?

Reality TV shows represent sites of rhetorical "struggle and negotiation over the meanings of race"; audience members performatively spectate race "in ways that reinforce or correspond to [their] own social and cultural reality" and predispositions.[14] Fan commentary on *Survivor* Sucks provides a critical entryway to examine how some audience members use racist iconography to assert their worldview of race and race relations. I turn my attention to three tropes of racist interpretation that some *Big Brother* viewers repeatedly cite when they discuss houseguests of color. These stereotypes include tropes of the monkey, monster, and exotic.

Trope of the Monkey

O'Brien observes that, "The dehumanization of 'out-groups' is often fostered through widespread use of animalistic metaphors to describe group members."[15] Animal-oriented name-calling directed at people of color pulls from 200 years of racist animal iconography, wherein racial and ethnic minorities in the United States have been compared to monkeys,[16] dogs, alligator bait,[17] and mules[18] in speeches, pieces of art, news media, cartoons, literature, and TV shows. Animal metaphors dehumanize and otherize houseguests of color.

Verbal communication and images suggesting that Black men and women are ape-like play into an entrenched stereotype that people of color, especially those of African descent, are the intellectual equivalent to monkeys.[19] Members of the antebellum South often relied on the Black-as-monkey motif to justify slavery and other horrific forms of institutionalized prejudice and violence. Nineteenth-century scientists like Ernst Haeckel fallaciously constructed a direct link between Black people and monkeys, and then used the connection to rationalize a theory of social Darwinism and so-called scientific racism. Figure 4.2.a is an image from Haeckel's book *The Evolution of Man* wherein the biologist pictorially represents a direct relationship between Black people and simians. In the past 200 years, racist, dehumanizing connections between people of color and monkeys have repeatedly emerged in multiple forms of U.S. discourse, including nineteenth-century posters that castigate Federal attempts to help freed slaves during the United States' Reconstruction era (see Figure 4.2.b), Internet memes that suggest Black infants are baby monkeys (see Figure 4.2.c), and Photoshopped images that digitally combine Michelle and Barack Obama's faces with the titular characters from *Planet of the Apes* (see Figure 4.2.d).

FIGURE 4.2 In clockwise order: a) image from 1874's *The Evolution of Man*;[20] b) nineteenth-century poster critiquing the Freedman's Bureau;[21] c) racist Internet meme comparing Black children to monkeys;[22] and d) racist Photoshopped image of President and First Lady Obama as simian-like creatures from *The Planet of the Apes*[23]

100 Houseguests of Color

Many *Survivor* Sucks participants perpetuate hateful and degrading associations between people of color and apes. These viewers constantly and unapologetically cite the monkey trope when discussing *Big Brother 13*'s sole Black female houseguest, Kalia. Kalia's comment thread on *Survivor* Sucks is titled "Kalia Kong," a reference that connects her name to a giant ape first popularized in the 1933 film *King Kong*. In her message thread alone, fans of the show replaced Kalia's name with Kong 1,205 times. A user named CourtCat writes, "Kong is digging through the fridge and cupboards like a ravenous rat."[24] Sprangensplet jokes, "Konglia probably gained 10 pounds in 24 hours."[25] Blatantly Oblivious even works racist monkey imagery into lyrics of a child's song. His post reads:

> One day a man too dumb to know the danger/
> Made a partner of this D-sized booby stranger/
> And the life they lead in the *Big Brother* home/
> Became the legend, the legend of/
> Kalia Kong, you know the name of Kalia Kong
> You know the fame of Kalia Kong/
> Eats 10 times as much as man.[26]

CourtCat, Sprangensplet, Blatantly Oblivious, and countless other members of *Survivor* Sucks build upon a troubling history where, "by the nineteenth century, the ape, the monkey, and the orangutan had become the interchangeable counterparts, the next of kin, to blacks in pseudoscientific and literary texts."[27]

Other community members utilize the Kong allusion in their Photoshopped images of Kalia. Figure 4.3 is a fan-produced graphic in which Kalia's eyes are superimposed over King Kong's. Bold, black, capital letters read "KALIA KONG" in the upper left corner of the image. Figure 4.4 recreates an iconic scene from the original *King Kong* film where the beast stands atop the Empire State Building and swats away fighter planes. In the photo, Kalia's head replaces Kong's, and Rachel and Jordan, two, White *Big Brother 13* contestants, have their heads affixed to two planes attacking Kalia. Racial division depicted in Figure 4.4 highlights racist subtext of the 1933 movie. Robin Means Coleman, a professor of Afro-American Studies at the University of Michigan, argues that King Kong is a metaphor for "a big Black man, right? A big black ape who is absolutely obsessed with whiteness and particularly White women."[28] When the image was posted, Figure 4.4's racial juxtaposition mirrored *Big Brother 13*'s narrative drama. Of the five remaining players, Kalia was set in opposition to three White women (Rachel, Porsche, and Jordan). People of color were four of the first five competitors evicted from the *Big Brother 13* house. Figure 4.4 ironically suggests that, despite her dire position in the game, Kalia poses a herculean threat to two White women, both of whom entered the house with boyfriends and now work together in an alliance. The image plays on anti-Black sentiment that configures Black people as a threat to White women, even though historically White people have brutalized Black men and women.[29]

FIGURE 4.3 "Kalia Kong"[30]

FIGURE 4.4 Kalia depicted as King Kong atop a building[31]

FIGURE 4.5 Natalie and Lydia depicted as monkeys[32]

Monkey-oriented fan racism is not limited to Kalia. Visiting the *Survivor* Sucks fan forum reveals a disturbing pattern of racist iconography, where viewers have used visual depictions of the monkey trope to narratize contestants who are not White. In Figure 4.5, members of *Survivor* Sucks named BBBratt and Ilovety manipulate pictures of monkeys so that their faces look like *Big Brother 11*'s Natalie and Lydia, both of whom are women of color. Taken together, Figures 4.3, 4.4, and 4.5 suggest that Black and Latina houseguests are apelike. The visual references work like links in a performative chain—each picture building upon the one it followed and collectively manufacturing a racist worldview where Black women and Latinas are subhuman and obstacles White players must defeat on their way to victory.

In their study of Black-ape analogs, Goff, Eberhardt, Williams, and Jackson demonstrate that historical representations linking Black people and monkeys continue to influence cognitive processes in the United States. The authors show that, "this Black-ape association alters visual perception and attention, and it increases endorsement of violence against Black" people.[33] In the context of *Big Brother*, monkey tropes shape perceptions of contestants from racially marginalized groups and constrain many viewers' idea of which players deserve to win and which competitors deserve fan ire.

Trope of the Exotic

Monkey analogs are closely associated with rhetoric that exoticizes, or fetishizes, people of color. Exoticization occurs when the habits, talents, phenotypic features and other characteristics of people of color are staged as radically different, foreign, and excessive. Stuart Hall describes racial exoticization as the "spectacle of the other." "Black people," Hall argues, have historically been "reduced to the signifiers of their physical appearance—thick lips, fuzzy hair, broad face and nose, and so on."[34] Hall turns to visual depictions of Black people in Victorian-era drawings, advertisements, cartoons, and commodities to illustrate his point. A nineteenth-century print ad for Pears Soap, for example, intimates that the "White man's burden" involves "brightening the dark corners of the earth" by way of its "ideal toilet soap." The ad's visual component includes a White child bathing his Black counterpart. After the Black kid exits the soapy bath, the parts of his skin soaked in Pears Soap have turned white. "Soap," Hall continues:

> symbolized the "racializing" of the domestic world and "domestication" of the colonial world. In its capacity to cleanse and purify, soap acquired, in the fantasy world of imperial advertising, the quality of fetish-object. It apparently had the power to wash black skin white, while at the same time keeping the imperial body clean and pure in the racially polluted contact zones "out there" in the Empire.[35]

A similar racist ideology is featured in a Fairies Soap advertisement, in which a White girl suggests that her Black shoeless friend should have her mother wash

104 Houseguests of Color

her with Fairies Soap (see Figure 4.6.a). The racist insinuation is that the product will purify the Black child by whitening her skin. White supremacy is contingent upon the myth that White and Black are in binary opposition, and that whiteness is normal, clean, pure, and good, while blackness is foreign, dirty, impure, and bad.

A comparable sort of racial exoticization emerges in the *Survivor* Sucks forum when *Big Brother* fans talk about women of color. Take, for example, fan notes about *Big Brother 11* contestant Natalie. The title of the Argentinian and Black woman's comment thread is, "Natalie: Discharge, Skidmarks, Ignored, Rejected, Dejected All-Around Loser." Posts in the forum include, "I hate this dirty, smelly looking bitch. She can bathe four times a day and still look filthy";[36] "one would think the massive amounts of fumes rising from this dirty troll would cause her to pass out but I guess if you sniff shit long enough it would burn out your olfactory senses";[37] "loving the hate for this dirty, dirty person! She has the mannerisms of so many types of animals. If she thinks it is ok to wear undies that have shit stains [and] vag discharge, you know she must have dingle berries and [a] possible yeast infection";[38] and, "I'm still trying to figure out how it is possible that she continues to look dirty even after she takes a shower."[39] As the season progressed, forum participants nicknamed her Gnatalie, a pun suggesting she is like an insect that breeds when people have not cleaned their garbage disposals.

Season 11's Photochop thread unsurprisingly contains pictures of Natalie resembling the nineteenth-century soap ads Stuart Hall critiques. In Figure 4.6.b, *Survivor* Sucks user UNCDavid shares an image of Jordan and Kevin styling Natalie's hair. A man wearing a clothespin on his nose is digitally manipulated into the photo. Text reading "Dirty Jobs" sits directly above Natalie's head as she gazes into the bathroom mirror. Figure 4.6.c depicts Natalie's Head-of-Household bedroom. When a player wins HoH, production styles the room to fit the contestant's taste. The viewer reworks Natalie's bedroom so that a heap of trash covers the floor, graffiti adorns the wall, and feral animals sit on her bed. The bottom of the image includes the text, "There goes the neighborhood."

"There goes the neighborhood," echoes a racist and classist era of White flight, or incidences where, "Whites fled from neighborhoods as Blacks bought homes there."[44] Filmed on the same lot as iconic television shows like *Gilligan's Island* (a program where seven White people live alone on an island), *My Three Sons* (a sitcom where four White men live in an almost exclusively White neighborhood), and *Falcon Crest* (a soap opera that chronicles the daily drama of a White family nestled away in a California vineyard), the *Big Brother* house is embedded in a televisual neighborhood that has capitalized on all-White fantasy worlds. Houseguests of color entering the neighborhood shatter the fiction of impenetrable whiteness.

Exoticization also emerges in simpler ways, like exaggerating perceived differences between the bodies and behaviors of Black and White houseguests. Less imaginative racist imagery on *Survivor* Sucks amplifies the size of Black women's lips (see Figure 4.7) and digitally manipulates photos so that Black women's bodies are excessive in size. Kalia's face was repeatedly superimposed on images

FIGURE 4.6 In clockwise order: a) Fairy Soap advertisement;[40] b) *Survivor* Sucks fan image suggesting Natalie is dirty;[41] and c) another fan-produced "Photochop" intimating Natalie is excessively unclean[42]

FIGURE 4.7 "Chima Lips"[43]

of corpulent men and women of color (see Figure 4.8). Fan images distort the dimensions of Kalia's average-sized body and place it in a performative space where her flesh is carnivalized. In her critical reflection of nineteenth-century freak show attraction Sarah Baartman, Carole Boyce Davies argues that depictions of Black women's bodies must be placed in the appropriate semiotic field. Davies asserts that "particular contexts of representation have to be historical as much as they have to be culturally located."[45] Similarly, photos posted on *Survivor* Sucks do not exist in a cultural vacuum and need to be considered in a wider socio-historical context. Davies advocates triangulated readings of Black female bodies. Triangular representations call attention to how depictions of Black women like Chima and Kalia are always embedded in a socio-historical network of symbols, commodity, and distortion.

Houseguests of Color **107**

FIGURE 4.8 In clockwise order: a) "Mooseknuckle";[46] b) a reworked image from the film *Norbit*;[47] c) "Playcow";[48] and d) Kalia as the Kool-Aid man[49]

The four photos that comprise Figure 4.8 represent a few of the ways fans of the show cite and reiterate stereotypes of Black women's bodies. In Figures 4.8.a, 4.8.b, and 4.8.c, Kalia's reworked physique is elevated to an arena of carnival-like exhibition. All three fan-produced images hyperbolize Kalia's weight and hypersexualize her flesh. The "Mooseknuckle" photo calls attention to a narratized version of Kalia's labia majora. Regardless of intent, the photo's creator echoes Victorian-era notions that a Black woman's overdeveloped labia symbolize her presumed savage and bestial nature. Exoticizing Kalia's genitals and making her appear abnormally large center and normalize whiteness by exaggerating Kalia's physicality. In Figure 4.8.d, Courtcat's racist insinuation is that Kalia's body is cartoonishly spherical, or pitcher-like; and presumably, because Kalia is Black, she drinks Kool-Aid, a beverage not even available in the *Big Brother* house.

Fans depictions of Kalia as gluttonous and self-indulgent sharply contrasts with Season 11's White champ and fan-favorite Jordan. Producers and reporters often referenced Jordan's humble background and generosity. Two seasons prior, she used her winnings to buy her mother a house and donated money to her two cousins' college funds. The four pictures that comprise Figure 4.8 position Kalia to be the Black yin to Jordan's White yang. English scholar Andrea Elizabeth Shaw reasons that:

> Fatness in black women is a physiological feature that functions much like the jungle setting in a Tarzan movie or as Diana Ross' untamable hair—as an encoding of sexuality and arguably blackness. Superimposing fat onto the black female body doubles its representative status as the antithesis of white femininity, since the dominant perspective on fatness is Western culture replicates the view of what blackness is already understood as denoting: bodily indiscipline and rebellion.[50]

Fans of the program narratize a caricature of Kalia and other racially marginalized houseguests. The artwork referenced in this chapter demonstrates an impulse many viewers share to transform even the most mundane behaviors and traits of Black people into a minstrel show. Africana Philosophy scholar Stephen Nathan Haymes characterizes this instinct as "white culture's exotic interest in black culture," which is an interest guided by "the white racist imagination."[51]

The Trope of Monstrosity

Using bestial or exotic themes to otherize houseguests of color builds upon White supremacist myths that White people are superior to other races and should therefore assert their cultural dominance; or, in this context, White houseguests are better than Black and Latina competitors and are inherently more likely to win and less deserving of fan scrutiny and criticism. This double-standard contextualizes why heterosexual White men like Season 8 winner "Evel" Dick are celebrated for sustained abusive behavior and contestants like Kalia and Natalie are castigated for relatively mundane outbursts. It bears repeating that no Black or Latin@ contestant has ever won *Big Brother's* grand prize and 16 of the show's 17 champions have been White. Producers and fans of *Big Brother* frequently paint contestants of color as 1) expendable, 2) obstacles that White competitors must conquer on their way to victory (return to Figure 4.4), and self-sacrificing characters who offer their own "symbolic annihilation . . . in the course of saving Whiteness."[52]

Perhaps no other trope of racial representation dehumanizes contestants of color more than monstrosity. In mass media, "the representation of monstrous difference typically functions to highlight the favorable, enlightened traits of White characters."[53] Comparing Kalia to *Star Wars'* Jabba the Hutt (see Figure 4.9.a), for instance, positions her as the show's antagonist and digitally reconstructs her body as morbidly obese, alien, and monstrous. The image, though, says much more about its creator than its subject. Reflecting on the use of monster metaphors in relation to Black people, Elizabeth Young contends that images of monstrous Blackness are not an account of "innate monstrosity but of being made monstrous

FIGURE 4.9 In clockwise order: a) "Kalia the Hut [sic]";[56] Lydia as *Hellraiser*'s Pinhead;[57] Natalie as *Friday the 13th*'s Jason and Lydia as *Nightmare on Elm Street*'s Freddy[58]

by the views of others."[54] Young's argument affirms the spectator-centric model of media criticism I advocate in this book. Audience members' performative impulses may be less filtered and self-conscious when they create and anonymously post art. Because the racist, monstrous images referenced in this chapter emerged organically and spontaneously on a *Big Brother* fan site, they likely provide an unfettered view of some audience members' attitudes about race. The art they anonymously post is not weighed down by social desirability bias, or the tendency for research respondents to underreport socially undesirable activities and beliefs, like racism.[55] Using performative spectatorship enables critics to mitigate response bias in qualitative media studies.

Fans of the show do not limit monster analogs to Black houseguests. Some viewers relied on horror motifs to narratize *every* woman of color on *Big Brother 11*. Spectators transformed *Big Brother 11*'s Natalie and Lydia into monsters from scary movies. In Figure 4.9.b, *Survivor* Sucks contributor ArtMaggot places Lydia's face over the demonic villain of the *Hellraiser* films. ArtMaggot's narratization of Lydia may have been in part goaded by production's edit of the CBS program. One episode of *Big Brother 11* contains a segment where Lydia fawns over a bodybuilder and fellow houseguest named Jessie. The clip begins with a close-up shot of the moon, which is a visual homage to horror films. Jarring music reminiscent of a scary movie plays in the background as Lydia makes her way to Jessie's bedroom as he sleeps. Producers use night-vision cameras to capture Lydia staring at Jessie in his darkened Head-of-Household bedroom. "I like watching Jessie when he sleeps," she confesses. Three sharp jabs of high-pitched piano keys punctuate Lydia's statement and highlight the illusion of her instability. Green-and-black tones of night-vision cameras and chilling music feed into the perception that Lydia is a dangerous woman.

In Figure 4.9.c, a participant in the same forum edits the poster for the scary movie *Freddy vs. Jason* so that Natalie represents *Friday the 13th*'s Jason and Lydia takes the place of *Nightmare on Elm Street*'s Freddy. The fan-produced images display notable racial and gender inversions, where homicidal White men in slasher films are replaced by women of color. This transposal belies socio-historical circumstances wherein White men have brutalized women of color and horror movie tropes where characters of color are often the first to be killed. *Big Brother 11*'s Photochop thread on *Survivor* Sucks contains 110 pages of fan-manufactured photos; and each page contains 20 posts. White houseguests are rarely portrayed as monsters in the thread's 2,200 entries. Fans depict White competitors as saints (e.g., Michele as "St. Michele"), Jesus (e.g., Jessie hanging on a crucifix), popular children's toys (e.g., Jordan as Rainbow Brite), superheroes (e.g., Jessie as BioJock and Superman), action-movie protagonists (e.g., Jessie as *Terminator 2*'s android hero), and warriors spearing the heads of interracial contestants. Conversely, spectators portray *Big Brother 11*'s contestants of color as witches (e.g., Lyida, Chima, and Natalie hovered over a boiling cauldron), aliens (e.g., Lydia as E.T.), terrorists (e.g., Russell as a Guantanamo prisoner), monsters from ancient Greek mythology (e.g., Lydia as Medusa), demonic entities (e.g., Chima as Pennywise from Stephen King's *It* and Samara from the movie *The Ring*), monkeys, sexually transmitted diseases (e.g., Lydia's head shooting out of a deformed penis), and pieces of fecal matter (e.g., Natalie's face placed on feces and Chima stuck in a toilet bowl). The repeated insinuation is that White players are heroes and competitors of color are subhuman and evil.

Racial juxtaposition illuminates racist hierarchies that govern many viewers' perceptions of houseguests of color and their White counterparts. *Big Brother*'s women of color are frequently depicted as shapeshifting werewolf women who "highlight the whiteness [of other performers] through physical transformation to a darker Other."[59] When contestants of color show anger, some fans are quick to narratize a bifurcated, werewolf-like tale for the houseguest; he or she is transformed into a "human divided against itself, unable to control its emotions or its body, and often amnesic in the aftermath of such episodes."[60] Figure 4.10 is a GIF, or animated image, where Chima's rage is portrayed in the same manner as a

FIGURE 4.10 Animated picture of Chima transforming into an undead monster[61]

112 Houseguests of Color

werewolf's. At any moment, tranquility may give way to animal-like fury. The GIF underscores the creator's perception of Chima's violent, werewolf-like transition.

Fan renderings of Chima were likely incited by how producers represented her in *Big Brother*'s CBS edit. Chima became incensed after fan-favorite Jeff won a special power called the Coup d'Etat. Producers presented the handsome, all-American White man with the Coup d'Etat after U.S. viewers unsurprisingly voted for him to win it. Unlike the powers Chima earned by winning the week's HoH competition, Jeff literally did not have to do anything but be White, handsome, and likable to hijack Chima's Head-of-Household reign. The Coup d'Etat allowed Jeff to nullify and replace Chima's Head-of-Household nominations. Jeff then used the Coup d'Etat to nominate two of Chima's closest allies in the house. The following week, Chima staged several acts of rebellion against production. She covered cameras with blankets, refused to go to the Diary Room when called to do so, and eventually threw her microphone pack into the hot tub. Producers finally decided to intervene and unceremoniously remove Chima from the *Big Brother* house and eliminate her from the competition.

Contestants from historically marginalized groups are regularly treated as rule breakers when they insist their opponents operate under the same strictures that govern their behavior. Chima rebelled because production hijacked a week of power she rightfully earned to advance the game of a popular White contestant. To make matters worse, *Big Brother* is already structured to favor White houseguests (e.g., most competitors and viewers are White).

The week Chima was evicted, producers created an edited package for the CBS show exclusively dedicated to *her* rule breaking. The montage opens with fan-favorite and eventual Season 11 champion Jordan narrating Chima's indiscretions. CBS painted Jordan as America's sweetheart and dubbed her romantic relationship with Coup d'Etat-winner Jeff as "one of *Big Brother*'s most adorable showmances."[62] The blond-haired, mild-mannered, White woman from North Carolina provided a convenient racial juxtaposition when CBS needed somebody to narrate Chima's supposed misdeeds. Jordan claims, "Chima is a diva. She's been breaking rules since day one. She acts like the rules don't apply to her." Producers then provide a montage of Chima "breaking rules since day one." On days six and ten, she does not immediately go to the Diary Room when production calls for her. On day 35, she correctly prophesizes that Jeff won a mysterious power and will use it to circumvent her HoH powers. The assortment of clips concludes with Chima's final week in the house, when she obstructs a camera and damages her microphone.

In my season, many of my roommates did not immediately go to the Diary Room when instructed to do so. Rule-breaking is a common occurrence in the house. One of my fellow competitors was nicknamed "fridge face" because, whenever he was a Have-Not, he buried his face in the fridge and ate food that was off limits to people on dietary restrictions for the week. Another contestant used pretzels to leave a message for her boyfriend, despite production's strict rules against writing. From my perspective, producers cobbled together clips of mundane, commonplace offenses and then used them to establish a pattern of bad behavior. The irony is that Chima only became recalcitrant after producers altered the competition in a manner that favored a White player who the game's structure already benefits. The favoritism was in fact so stark that Chima could forecast who specifically would win the game-changing power and predict that it would negatively affect the HoH powers she earned. But in the world of manufactured reality, Chima is the one "breaking rules" and the contestant who "doesn't think the rules apply to her." Chima's storyline is a fitting but frustrating allegory for institutionalized racism in the United States, especially in the context of mass media.

Big Brother's Manufactured Silence as Complicit, Systemic Racism

Reality TV producers may value racial diversity because their programming relies on the sort of "human drama that unfolds when people from diverse backgrounds—based on race, ethnicity, socioeconomic, age, religion, and sexual orientation—interact with one another."[63] Racial diversity, unfortunately, does not necessarily result in producers addressing racism people of color encounter while filming a reality TV show. Moreover, when producers tackle racist subject matter, they "repeatedly depict racism as a matter of personal belief situated in rural conservatives, which downplays structural aspects of racism and suggests that its solution is to be found in the education of ignorant individuals."[64]

Casting people of color but failing to include moments of racism they endure in the *Big Brother* house is a form of structural racism characteristic of the reality TV genre. In her scholarly consideration of *The Bachelor*, Rachel Dubrofsky points out that, season after season, women of color are included in the cast but remain largely irrelevant to the program's storylines. Durbofsky suggests that, "The series invites us to consider race within the logic of relational choice, rather than within the logic of representation or production."[65] In other words, how might production neglecting to include racism in *Big Brother*'s primetime narrative function as structural, or institutionalized, racism?

Big Brother's fifteenth season offers a compelling entryway to investigate production's racist complicity. Season 15 featured 16 houseguests, including two Black competitors, one Korean contestant, and thirteen White players. The season took an early and uncomfortable turn when, in the game's first week, Internet viewers reported multiple instances of racist and homophobic speech uttered by several of the season's White, heterosexual participants. Three White women named Aaryn, GinaMarie, and Amanda were among the season's worst offenders. Aaryn referred to Korean player Helen as "Asian eyes" and made statements like, "Shut up and go make some rice." She also used a hyperbolized Korean accent in yellow-face impersonations of Asian women. Aaryn's ally GinaMarie suggested punching Helen in the face might "make her eyes straight."

114 Houseguests of Color

Racist hate speech was a hot news topic in June of 2013. The same month *Big Brother 15* premiered, the media obsessively detailed accounts of celebrity chef Paula Deen making derogatory comments about Black people. Deen's speech resulted in the cancelation of her Food Network television show and the end of lucrative deals with Walmart, Target, J.C. Penney, Sears, Kmart, and QVC. Deen's racist spectacle positioned *Big Brother*'s producers to construct a story about racist animus that emerged in Season 15. Producers unfortunately failed to tackle racism and homophobia in the early weeks of CBS's *Big Brother* broadcast. Turning a blind eye to racism, sexism, and homophobia made producers complicit in the hate speech they actively denied.

Outraged, I penned an open letter to *Big Brother*'s production team and posted it on my blog on June 30, 2013. The entry reads:

> Houseguests GinaMarie, Aaryn, and Katlin referred to historically marginalized players as "tokens." Sadly, they aren't too far off in their assessment. Characters like Andy, Candice, Howard, and Helen are reduced to mere tokens when production fails to include micro-aggressions that they endure on a day-to-day basis. What's the point of casting racial, ethnic, and sexual minorities if production's going to edit out the racism, ethnic discrimination, and homophobia that these people encounter inside the house? It would be irresponsible to punt this issue. What makes Aaryn's homophobia and racism especially insidious is that it comes packaged in a bright-eyed, pageant-like exterior. I mean, how can somebody so sweet looking spew so much venom? Viewers would have to see it to believe it.

Within a week, the *New York Times*, *Los Angeles Times*, *People*, and the *Hollywood Reporter* featured portions of my critique in stories about *Big Brother 15*'s manufactured absence of racism and homophobia. Brian Stelter of the *New York Times* speaks to production's contrived omission of hate speech when he explains that:

> The slurs were shown on the Internet (where paying subscribers watch live feeds from the house around the clock—"See what we can't show you on TV," the CBS Web site says) but were not immediately on the television version of the show, whose producers distill the action into three hourly episodes each week. This troubled some loyal followers of *Big Brother*, because television viewers were seeing an incomplete picture of the participants. On a show with a $500,000 grand prize, perceptions and reputations are important.[66]

Cultural conversations about newsmaking racist speech quickly shifted away from Paula Deen and to *Big Brother*.

The longer CBS ignored the controversy in *Big Brother*'s narrative, the larger viewer outrage grew: 27,000 fans of the program signed an online petition asking CBS to expel Aaryn from the house. The network finally acquiesced and aired Aaryn's comments on its July 7 *Big Brother* broadcast. Soon thereafter and for the first time in the show's 15-season history, each episode started with a disclaimer that read:

> *Big Brother* is a reality show about a group of people who have no privacy 24/7. At times, the houseguests may reveal prejudices and other beliefs that CBS does not condone. Views or opinions expressed by a houseguest are those of the individuals speaking and do not represent the views or opinions of CBS.

One can only speculate whether CBS would have included racism in its Season 15 narrative had fans of the show and journalists not intervened and pressured them to do so. It is, however, undeniable that, in the summer of 2013, *Big Brother*'s spectators proved to be more than passive consumers of entertainment. Thousands of Internet viewers actively participated in the show's production by highlighting hateful comments CBS left on the cutting-room floor for two weeks.

Although CBS started to include bigotry in its broadcasts, they did little to prevent hate speech in the house. Season 15's lowest moment occurred when Aaryn moved a Black houseguest's mattress from its frame to the floor as two other White women cackled. When Candice, the only Black woman in the house, confronted the trio about Aaryn's prank, Aaryn snapped her fingers, rolled her shoulders, and mimicked Black speech dialects. The White woman from Texas mockingly asked Candice, "Whatchu gon' do gurl? Where's yo' class?" Aaryn's friend GinaMarie chimed in with, "You want the Black to come out?" Once Candice left the room, GinaMarie claimed Candice "is on the dark side, but she's already dark," prompting Aaryn to respond, "Be careful what you say in the dark because you might not be able to see the bitch."

Several other *Big Brother 15* houseguests engaged in acts of racist and homophobic antagonism, yet their vitriol was largely left unaired on CBS. *Big Brother 15* contestant Amanda, for instance, called gay competitor Andy "faggoty Ann," said Candice's hair is "greasy and nappy," characterized Helen (a Korean) as "the fucking Chinaman," and referred to "the black guy, the Asian, and the gay guy" as the "three outcasts." CBS shockingly made Amanda the primary narrator and in-house critic of Aaryn's racism. Producers even edited and broadcast a package where Amanda confronts Aaryn about her racist animus. CBS failed to air footage where Amanda backpedals and tells Aaryn that she does not think she is racist and claims Candice and Howard play the "race card" to get ahead in the game. By creating stories where racism is extraordinary and relegated to a single person in the house, *Big Brother* obscures the ways in which racism is a common, ordinary, and everyday phenomenon.

116 Houseguests of Color

Performative Spectatorship as Activism

Up until this point, I have focused largely on the ways in which *Big Brother*'s viewers utilize performative spectatorship to perpetuate stereotypes about people from historically marginalized groups. Season 15's controversy provided an opportunity for fans to resist racism and other forms of bigotry via performative spectatorship. Throughout the season, many fans pointed out that Aaryn is an anagram for Aryan and described her as "KKK Barbie." Calling Aaryn Aryan reconfigures her name so that it is linked to Nazi ideologies of White superiority and racial hierarchy. Fans titled her *Survivor* Sucks thread, "Aryan: Racist Narcissist with a Busted Hat:'Who Wants to See my KKK Room?'" One viewer active on the forum asks, "Was she raised by neo-Nazis? I wonder if the whole 'Aaryn = Aryan anagram was a subtle reference by her parents when naming her."[67] Another user writes, "Aryan's a pretty girl. She can certainly find a rich Klan daddy."[68]

Fans of the show also created numerous Photoshopped images of the more overtly racist *Big Brother 15* houseguests. *Survivor* Sucks user Django posted Figure 4.11.a to the season's "Photochop" thread. Aaryn's head is placed on the body of World War II icon Rosie the Riveter. Django alters Rosie's famous catchphrase, "We can do it!" so that it reads, "We Klan do it!" Klan is, of course, a synecdochical reference to the U.S.-based White supremacist group, the Ku Klux Klan. The Klan's emblem is pasted to the lapel of Aaryn's shirt. Figure 4.11.b is a fan-produced image of GinaMarie and Aaryn as a team on CBS reality series *The Amazing Race*. The viewer has reworked the show's title so that it reads, "The Amazing Racists." In Figure 4.11.c, *Survivor* Sucks participant ArtMaggot reimagines an oft-referenced scene from 1957, when nine high school students were among the first Black people to integrate into Little Rock's public school system. One of the more memorable and disturbing photos from the event features a group of White men and women trailing behind a Black high school student named Elizabeth Eckford. A 15-year-old White woman named Hazel Massery screams at Eckford. Reporters at the event noted that the White demonstrators behind Eckford yelled, "Lynch her! Lynch her!" "Go home, nigger!" and, "No nigger bitch is going to get in our school."[73] Aaryn's face is placed over Massery's in the digitally manipulated image. ArtMaggot jokes that the picture is one of "Aaryn's family photos." Figure 4.11.d includes GinaMarie and Aaryn standing in front of a sign that reads, "We want White tenants in our White community." Aaryn's face is covered by a Ku Klux Klan hood. A Nazi arm patch wraps around her left bicep.

Earlier in this chapter, I referenced the work of Carole Boyce Davies, who advocates placing contemporary images in a socio-historical network of figures. Historical triangulation helps contextualize symbols by highlighting the ways in which pieces of art—both high (i.e., art found in a museum) and low (e.g., photos posted to *Survivor* Sucks)—function as ongoing, citational, and culturally sedimented ideology. Images that parody iconic photographs potentially transcend their historical allusions, gain "meaning from subsequent symbolic associations,"

Houseguests of Color   117

FIGURE 4.11 In clockwise order: a) "We Klan do It!";[69] b) "The Amazing Racists";[70] c) "Aaryn Family Photos";[71] and d) "We Want White Tenants in Our White Community"[72]

and "reaffirm the identity of the body politic."[74] Figures 4.11.a, 4.11.c, and 4.11.d situate Aaryn's and GinaMarie's racist speech acts in a larger field of historically significant and culturally recognizable images of U.S.-based racism. The secondary texts work in conjunction to repeatedly and forcefully contend that Aaryn's and GinaMarie's behavior is regressive and inconsistent with today's cultural values. The suggestion, to modify Figure 4.11.d, is that some *Big Brother* fans do not want racist houseguests in their virtual community.

Peculiarly, most *Survivor* Sucks participants turn a blind eye to racism and homophobia that emerges from the site's membership. Few people in the forum acknowledge, let alone critique, repeated depictions of Black people as apes or women of color as dirty or bad mothers. This emergent inconsistency is a form of racist victimage, or scapegoating, whereby Aaryn and GinaMarie "serve as scapegoats in a [digital] society that 'purifies itself' by 'moral indignation' in condemning them."[75] Ott and Aoki point out that scapegoating represents a speaker's iniquities because "symbolic forms that manage guilt can only be 'successful if the audience is guilty of the sins portrayed in the discourse.'"[76] Many Season 15 viewers used Aaryn and GinaMarie as vessels to purge their own sense of racist guilt. Reality TV producers often encourage racist scapegoating among viewers by representing racism as an individual prerogative or character default in a select individual rather than a more insidious and systemic cultural phenomenon. The hope is that houseguests like Aaryn and GinaMarie will go home, view their behavior on the program, and rehabilitate. Fans of the show sometimes use moral instruction to justify their brutal treatment of contestants after a season has concluded. "I can't wait for [these houseguests] to see what people really think of them,"[77] is a common sentiment articulated in the *Survivor* Sucks message threads. Some viewers frame harassment of past competitors as an honorable corrective. The problem is that scapegoating enables spectators to assert a sense of racist innocence by placing their guilt in another agent. *They* (Aaryn and GinaMarie) are guilty of racism; *we* are innocent and must rehabilitate them.

This is not to say that viewer critiques of racism cannot also be positive and productive. Unlike simulacra that stereotypes gay contestants and houseguests of color, Figures 4.11.a through 4.11.d have the potential to work in an activist manner. In his analysis of Earth First! and Green Peace protest photos, rhetoric scholar Kevin DeLuca makes a case for the activist implications of what he calls "image events." DeLuca writes that:

> In today's televisual public sphere corporations and states stage spectacles certifying their status before the people/public *and* subaltern counterpublics participate through the performance of image events, employing the consequent publicity as a social medium through which to hold corporations and states accountable, help form public opinion, and constitute their own identities as subaltern counterpublics. Critique through spectacle, not critique versus spectacle.[78]

Fed up by CBS's silence regarding racism and homophobia in the *Big Brother* house, some viewers composed and posted art to social networks and fan forums. Their work helped generate publicity, or news items, about hate speech on the *Big Brother* set and perhaps influenced an initially reluctant major media conglomerate to address racist and homophobic behavior among Season 15's participants.

The fans' performative spectatorship also constitutes a form of media theory and criticism. Figures 4.11.a through 4.11.d are parodied allusions that "direct the audience's attention by the addition, omission, substitution, and/or distortion of visual elements."[79] *Big Brother* viewers act as cultural critics when they add a Klan emblem to Rosie the Riveter's shirt, substitute Aaryn for Hazel Massery, and distort the name *The Amazing Race* so that it reads "The Amazing Racists." The art functions as a performative intervention insofar as it reminds other viewers that racism is not only an act of personal prejudice but also systemic and intertwined in a socio-historical web of meaning and violence.

More than act as mere voyeurs of reality TV, members of *Survivor* Sucks co-construct meaning of the series and its players through the symbols they reference, manipulate, and create. In this sense, their work functions as what queer theorist Judith Halberstam might describe as low theory. Halberstam argues that, "Everyone participates in intellectual activity, just as they cook meals and mend clothes without necessarily being chefs or tailors."[80] High theory is the sort of dense, referential literature cited in scholarship and discussed in graduate school seminars. Low theory tends to eschew the sometimes confusing, abstract grammars of philosophy. High and low theory speak to distinct intellectual communities. I have argued elsewhere that, "Digital media may be considered 'lower' than more conventional forms of theory, inquiry, and high art; but, time and again, online rhetoric proves its consequentiality by being passed around by millions and critically dissected."[81] Low theory celebrates artifacts that come from silly, unconventional archives, or records that may otherwise be labeled "unserious." Placing a Klan hood over Aaryn's face or repeatedly referring to her as Aryan demonstrates how silly but critical responses to a mediated text may powerfully connect contemporary controversies to historical events. Fan art also influences other audience members' interpretation of hateful speech.

Aaryn's Eviction

On August 29, 2013, Aaryn was evicted from the *Big Brother* house by a unanimous vote. Like millions of other viewers, I could hardly wait for Julie Chen's exit interview with the cherub-faced Texan. The normally composed and impartial Julie spent the previous two months taking a stand against Aaryn's racism. On her morning talk show, Julie showed a montage of Aaryn's racist behavior and then remarked, "My heart is pounding. Am I the only one who feels so enraged? That's the third time I've watched that clip and it does not get any easier." Sweat poured down my forehead as Aaryn made her way from the front door of the *Big Brother* house to Julie. A mix of cheers, boos, and hisses welcomed her back to the "real" world. Julie dutifully shook Aaryn's hand and asked her to take a seat. "We have a lot to talk about, including the mixed reception you just got," Julie explained. Less than two minutes into the dialogue Julie pointed out that Aaryn had said "some pretty harsh things" about her fellow competitors. "Amanda even tried to warn you that some of your words—others were interpreting as racist," Julie declared. "How do you respond to that?"

"Being Southern, it's a stereotype, and I have said some things that have been taken completely out of context. I do not mean to ever come off as racist," Aaryn stammered. Members of the live audience laughed at her equivocation.

"We want to point out that everyone in the house went in knowing that everything they say, everything they do gets broadcast live on the Internet. Let me just read back a few of the things you said." Men and women in the audience gasped and the cadence of the Texan's breath became rapid as Julie quickly read an abbreviated list of Aaryn's offenses. An uncomfortable half-smile gripped the

120 Houseguests of Color

lower half of Aaryn's face. "I do not remember saying those things," Aaryn pleaded. The audience loudly groaned in a collective act of frustration and disbelief.

An odd, confusing feeling pulsed through me. I expected to enjoy Aaryn's proverbial moment of truth but Schadenfreude gave way to empathy. I did not like Aaryn, but I felt producers had unfairly made her the exclusive target of anti-racist anger. Julie even mentioned Amanda's attempt to curb Aaryn's racist speech but Amanda was hardly the social justice advocate CBS made her out to be. Producers had Amanda narrate Aaryn's racism and homophobia but, in the CBS broadcast, failed to include numerous moments Amanda engaged in racist and homophobic communication, like when she claimed the have-not shower was the "Puerto Rican shower" because "Puerto Ricans are smelly," said Candice was pulling the "race card," referred to Black contestant Howard as Black Mamba and the Dark Knight, suggested Candice smells like watermelon and Helen likes eggrolls, or called Andy "Kermit the fag" when he wore green shorts and an emerald shirt.

Julie diplomatically ended the interview by explaining to Aaryn, "You're in a unique spot, because when this is all over you're going to get to go home and watch a whole lot of yourself living for seventy days. After you watch all this footage, I think you might have a new perspective on things."

The greater lesson, though, is that viewers might recognize racism as systemic by watching Season 15. *Big Brother*'s producers missed an opportunity to theatrically depict racism as a cultural institution, rather than just a character flaw in a naïve woman from Texas, when they single-mindedly focused on two contestants' racist behavior. The conceit of reality television is that, even in its most spectacular moments, the genre reflects, or at least should mirror, the way everyday people think and interact, even when they are not being filmed. Julie's suggestion that Aaryn is in a unique spot to review her behavior circumvents the transformative potential of reality TV. In its best moments, the medium enables audiences to see themselves in the flaws of others, rather than use reality TV participants as scapegoats to purge cultural guilt.

Notes

1 Chimandie Ngozi Adichie, "To the First Lady, with Love," *The New York Times*, last modified October 17, 2016, accessed March 1, 2017, www.nytimes.com/2016/10/17/t-magazine/michelle-obama-chimamanda-ngozi-adichie-gloria-steinem-letter.html.
2 Patricia Hill Collins, *Black Sexual Politics: African Americans, Gender, and the New Racism* (New York, NY: Routledge, 2004), 147–8.
3 GinaF20697, "Libra: Whore, Slut, Skank," *Survivor Sucks*, July 13, 2008 http://survivorsucks.yuku.com/search/topic/topic/35554.
4 SurvivorArctic, "Libra: Whore, Slut, Skank," *Survivor Sucks*, July 13, 2008 http://survivorsucks.yuku.com/search/topic/topic/35554.
5 Riff, "BB10 Photochop," *Survivor Sucks*, August 10, 2008 http://survivorsucks.yuku.com/topic/34530/BB10-Photochop?page=49.
6 Richard L. Celsi, Randall L. Rose, and Thomas W. Leigh, "An Exploration of High-Risk Leisure Consumption through Skydiving," *Journal of Consumer Research* 20, no. 1 (1993): 1–23.

7 Adrianne Kunkel, Mary Lee Hummert, and Michael Robert Dennis, "Social Learning Theory: Modeling and Communication in the Family Context," *Engaging Theories in Family Communication: Multiple Perspectives*, ed. Dawn O. Braithwaite and Leslie A. Baxter (Thousand Oaks, CA: Sage), 260–75.

8 Rebecca Pardo, "Reality Television and the Metapragmatics of Racism," *Journal of Linguistic Anthropology* 23, no. 1 (2013): 65.

9 Mark P. Orbe, "Representations of Race in Reality TV: Watch and Discuss," *Critical Studies in Media Communication* 25, no. 4 (2008): 350.

10 Rachel E. Dubrofsky and Antoine Hardy, "Performing Race in Flavor of Love and the Bachelor," *Critical Studies in Media Communication* 25, no. 4 (2008): 373–92.

11 Debra C. Smith, "Critiquing Reality-Based Televisual Black Fatherhood: A Critical Analysis of Run's House and Snoop Dogg's Father Hood," *Critical Studies in Media Communication* 25, no. 4 (2008): 393–412.

12 Theodore O. Prosise and Ann Johnson, "Law Enforcement and Crime on Cops and World's Wildest Police Videos: Anecdotal Form and the Justification of Racial Profiling," *Western Journal of Communication* 68, no. 1 (2004): 72–91.

13 Mark Adrejevic and Dean Colby, "Racism and Reality TV: The Case of MTV's Road Rules," *How Real Is Reality TV? Essay on Representation and Truth*, ed. David S. Escoffery (Jefferson, NC: McFarland and Company, 2006), 195–211.

14 Katrina E. Bell-Jordan, "Black. White. and a Survivor of the Real World: Constructions of Race on Reality TV," *Critical Studies in Media Communication* 25, no. 4 (2008): 354.

15 Gerald V. O'Brien, "Indigestible Food, Conquering Hordes, and Waste Materials: Metaphors of Immigrants and the Early Immigration Restriction Debate in the United States," *Metaphor and Symbol* 18, no. 1 (2003): 42.

16 Yuval Taylor and Jake Austen, *Darkest America: Black Minstrelsy from Slavery to Hip-Hop* (New York, NY: W.W. Norton and Company, 2012).

17 Franklin Hughes, "Question of the Month: Alligator Bait," *Jim Crow Museum of Racist Memorabilia*, October 5, 2–13, www.ferris.edu/jimcrow/question/may13/index.htm.

18 Christopher E. Koy, "The Mule as Metaphor in the Fiction of Charles Waddell Chestnutt," *Theory and Practice in English Studies* 4 (2005): 93–100.

19 Ralina L. Joseph, "Imagining Obama: Reading Overtly and Inferentially Racist Images of Our 44th President, 2007–2008," *Communication Studies* 62, no. 4 (2011): 389–405.

20 Ernst Haeckel, "Anthropogenie" (1874), drawing, *The Evolution of Man*, www.helsinki.fi/~pjojala/Haeckel_illustrations.html.

21 "The Freedman's Bureau," illustration, *American Political Prints*, 1766–1876, 1866. From Library of Congress Prints and Photographs Division, accessed July 12, 2017, www.loc.gov/pictures/item/2008661698/.

22 "Facebook Refuses to Remove Racist 'Black Baby as Chimp' Post," *image, Clutch*, June 12, 2017, www.clutchmagonline.com/2013/02/facebook-refuses-to-remove-racist-black-baby-as-chimp-post/.

23 "Obama_liberynew," *image, Democrats Hall of Shame*, June 12, 2017, http://democratshallofshame.net/Gallery/Buckwheat_Pics_Gallery_2/index30.html.

24 CourtCat, "Kalia Kong: Leave the Food Area! Track Her Glutton Here," *Survivor Sucks*, July 17, 2011, http://survivorsucks.yuku.com/search/topic/topic/85019.

25 Sprangenspelt, "Kalia Kong: Leave the Food Area! Track Her Glutton Here," *Survivor Sucks*, July 17, 2011, http://survivorsucks.yuku.com/search/topic/topic/85019.

26 Blatantly Oblivious, "Kalia Kong: Leave the Food Area! Track Her Glutton Here," *Survivor Sucks*, July 19, 2011, http://survivorsucks.yuku.com/search/topic/topic/85019.

27 T. Denean Sharpley-Whitin, *Black Venus: Sexualized Savages, Primal Fears, and Primitive Narratives in French* (Durham, NC: Duke University Press, 1999), 24.

28 Gene Demby, "Can You Make a Movie with King Kong Without Perpetuating Racial Undertones," *NPR*, March 11, 2017, www.npr.org/2017/03/11/519845882/can-you-make-a-movie-with-king-kong-without-perpetuating-racial-undertones.

122 Houseguests of Color

29 Angela Davis, "Rape, Racism, and the Myth of the Black Rapist," *Feminism and 'Race'*, ed. Kum-Kum Bhavnani (New York, NY: Oxford University Press, 2001), 172–201.

30 Mds1978CA, "BB13: Official Photochop Thread," *Survivor Sucks*, July 27, 2011, http://survivorsucks.yuku.com/topic/84407/BB13-OFFICIAL-Photochop-Thread?page=38.

31 Gatorzzz Byars, "BB13: Official Photochop Thread," *Survivor Sucks*, September 2, 2011, http://survivorsucks.yuku.com/topic/84407/BB13-OFFICIAL-Photochop-Thread?page=56.

32 BBBratt, "BB11 Photo Chops," *Survivor Sucks*, August 16, 2009, http://survivorsucks.yuku.com/topic/53805/BB11-Photo-Chops?page=82; Ilovety, "BB11 Photo Chops," *Survivor Sucks*, August 8, 2009, http://survivorsucks.yuku.com/topic/53805/BB11-Photo-Chops?page=10.

33 Phillip Atiba Goff, Jennifer L. Eberhardt, Melissa J. Williams, and Jackson Matthew Christian, "Not Yet Human: Implicit Knowledge, Historical Dehumanization, and Contemporary Consequences," *Journal of Personality and Social Psychology* 94, no. 2 (2008): 292.

34 Stuart Hall, "The Spectacle of the Other," *Representation: Cultural Representations and Signifying Practices*, ed. Stuart Hall, Jessica Evans, and Sean Nixon (Thousand Oaks, CA: Sage, 2013), 249.

35 Ibid., 241.

36 Dizzie Lizzie57, "Natalie: Discharge, Skidmarks, Ignored, Rejected, Dejected All-Around Loser," *Survivor Sucks*, July 25, 2009, http://survivorsucks.yuku.com/search/topic/topic/54220.

37 LeeLeeRaRa, "Natalie: Discharge, Skidmarks, Ignored, Rejected, Dejected All-Around Loser," *Survivor Sucks*, August 8, 2009, http://survivorsucks.yuku.com/search/topic/topic/54220.

38 Dizzie Lizzie57, "Natalie: Discharge, Skidmarks, Ignored, Rejected, Dejected All-Around Loser," *Survivor Sucks*, August 13, 2009, http://survivorsucks.yuku.com/search/topic/topic/54220.

39 Russthorn, "Natalie: Discharge, Skidmarks, Ignored, Rejected, Dejected All-Around Loser," *Survivor Sucks*, August 16, 2009, http://survivorsucks.yuku.com/search/topic/topic/54220.

40 "Why Doesn't Your Mamma Wash You with Fairy Soap?" *1967 MGB GT: A Restoration and Historical Journal*, July 20, 2017, http://mgb1967.com/why-doesnt-your-mamma-wash-you-with-fairy-soap/why-doesnt-your-mamma-wash-you-with-fairy-soap/.

41 Uncdavid, "BB11 Photo Chops," *Survivor Sucks*, September 3, 2009, http://survivorsucks.yuku.com/topic/53805/BB11-Photo-Chops?page=99.

42 Uncdavid, "BB11 Photo Chops," *Survivor Sucks*, September 4, 2009, http://survivorsucks.yuku.com/topic/53805/BB11-Photo-Chops?page=100.

43 BBBratt, "BB11 Photo Chops," *Survivor Sucks*, August 13, 2009, http://survivorsucks.yuku.com/topic/53805/BB11-Photo-Chops?page=77.

44 Kevin M. Kruse, *White Flight: Atlanta and the Making of Modern Conservatism* (Princeton, NJ, Princeton University Press, 2013), 5.

45 Carole Boyce Davies, "Black/Female/Bodies Carnivalized in Spectacle and Space," *Black Venus 2010: They Called Her 'Hottentot'*, ed. Deborah Willis (Philadelphia: Temple University Press, 2010), 186.

46 CourtCat, "BB13: Official Photochop Thread," *Survivor Sucks*, July 17, 2011, http://survivorsucks.yuku.com/topic/84407/BB13-OFFICIAL-Photochop-Thread?page=19.

47 Princess, "BB13: Official Photochop Thread," *Survivor Sucks*, September 3, 2011, http://survivorsucks.yuku.com/topic/84407/BB13-OFFICIAL-Photochop-Thread?page=56.

48 Uncdavid, "BB13: Official Photochop Thread," *Survivor Sucks*, September 2, 2011, http://survivorsucks.yuku.com/topic/84407/BB13-OFFICIAL-Photochop-Thread? page=28.

49 CourtCat, "BB13: Official Photochop Thread," *Survivor Sucks*, August 9, 2011, http://survivorsucks.yuku.com/topic/84407/BB13-OFFICIAL-Photochop-Thread? page=42.

50 Andrea Elizabeth Shaw, *The Embodiment of Disobedience: Fat Black Women's Unruly Political Bodies* (Lanham, MD: Lexington Books), 50.

51 Stephen Nathan Haymes, *Race, Culture, and the City: A Pedagogy for Black Urban Struggle* (Albany, NY: State University of New York Press, 1995), 16.

52 Ibid., 151.

53 Robin R. Means Coleman, *Horror Noire: Blacks in American Horror Films from the 1890s to Present* (New York, NY: Routledge, 2011), 105.

54 Elizabeth Young, *Black Frankenstein: The Making of an American Metaphor* (New York, NY: New York University Press, 2008), 78.

55 Ivar Krumpal, "Determinants of Social Desirability Bias in Sensitive Surveys: A Literature Review," *Quality and Quantity* 47, no. 4 (2013): 2025–47.

56 Mds1978ca, "BB13: Official Photochop Thread," *Survivor Sucks*, August 11, 2011, http://survivorsucks.yuku.com/topic/84407/BB13-OFFICIAL-Photochop-Thread? page=44.

57 ArtMaggot, "BB11 Photo Chops," *Survivor Sucks*, July 26, 2009, http://survivorsucks. yuku.com/topic/53805/BB11-Photo-Chops?page=46.

58 Ilovety, "BB11 Photo Chops," *Survivor Sucks*, July 28, 2009, http://survivorsucks.yuku. com/topic/53805/BB11-Photo-Chops?page=49.

59 Bernadette M. Calafell, "Monstrous Femininity: Constructions of Women of Color in the Academy," *Journal of Communication Inquiry* 36, no. 2 (2012): 114.

60 Phillip A. Bernhardt-House, "The Werewolf as Queer, the Queer as Werewolf, and Queer Werewolves," *Queering the Non/Human*, ed. Norine Giffney and Myra J. Hird (Berlington, VT: Ashgate, 2008), 163.

61 CourtCat, "BB11 Photo Chops," *Survivor Sucks*, August 15, 2009, http://survivorsucks. yuku.com/topic/53805/BB11-Photo-Chops?page=80.

62 "Big Brother Sweethearts Jeff Schroeder and Jordan Lloyd Reveal the Gender of Their Baby," *CBS*, June 8, 2016, www.cbs.com/shows/big_brother/news/ 1005276/big-brother-sweethearts-jeff-schroeder-and-jordan-lloyd-reveal-gender-of-their-baby.

63 Mark P. Orbe, "Representations of Race in Reality TV," 349.

64 Ibid., 70.

65 Rachel Dubrofsky, "The Bachelor: Whiteness in the Harem," *Critical Studies in Media Communication* 23, no. 1 (2006): 42.

66 Brian Stelter, "Reality Show Contestants Pay a Real-World Price: "On Big Brother, Racial and Gay Slurs Abound," *New York Times*, July 8, 2013, www.nytimes. com/2013/07/09/business/media/on-big-brother-racial-and-gay-slurs-abound. html.

67 Zingbot9000, "Aryan: Racist Narcissist with a Busted Hat: 'Who Wants to See my KKK Room?'" *Survivor Sucks*, July 4, 2013 http://survivorsucks.yuku.com/search/ topic/topic/114198/q/aryan?page=2.

68 Marnie Edgar, "Aryan: Racist Narcissist with a Busted Hat: 'Who Wants to See my KKK Room?'" *Survivor Sucks*, July 13, 2013, http://survivorsucks.yuku.com/search/ topic/topic/114198/q/aryan?page=5.

69 Django, "BB15 Official Photochop Thread," *Survivor Sucks*, July 18, 2013, http://survivorsucks.yuku.com/topic/114201/BB15-OFFICIAL-Photochop-Thread? page=18.

70 PassThePaxil, "BB15 Official Photochop Thread," *Survivor Sucks*, October 1, 2013, http://survivorsucks.yuku.com/topic/114201/BB15-OFFICIAL-Photochop-Thread?page=39.

71 ArtMaggot, "BB15 Official Photochop Thread," *Survivor Sucks*, July 12, 2013, http://survivorsucks.yuku.com/topic/114201/BB15-OFFICIAL-Photochop-Thread?page=14.

72 Talk, "BB15 Official Photochop Thread," *Survivor Sucks*, July 14, 2013, http://survivorsucks.yuku.com/topic/114201/BB15-OFFICIAL-Photochop-Thread?page=15.

73 David Margolick, "Elizabeth Eckford and Hazel Bryan: The Story Behind the Photograph that Shamed America," *The Telegraph*, October 9, 2011, www.telegraph.co.uk/news/worldnews/northamerica/8813134/Elizabeth-Eckford-and-Hazel-Bryan-the-story-behind-the-photograph-that-shamed-America.html.

74 Janis L. Edwards and Carol K. Winkler, "Representative Form and the Visual Ideograph: The Iwo Jima Image in Editorial Cartoons," *Quarterly Journal of Speech* 83, no. 3 (1997): 302–303.

75 Kenneth Burke, *A Grammar of Motives* (New York, NY: Prentice Hall, 1945), 406.

76 Brian L. Ott and Eric Aoki, "The Politics of Negotiating Public Tragedy: Media Framing of the Matthew Shepard Murder," *Rhetoric & Public Affairs* 5, no. 3 (2002): 490; Barry Burmmett, "Burkean Comedy and Tragedy, Illustrated in Reactions to the Arrest of John Delorean," *Central States Speech Journal* 35 (1984): 218.

77 JoHnNyBLuE725, "BB19: Ongoing LIVE FEED Discussion/Commentary," *Survivor Sucks*, September 4, 2017, www.tapatalk.com/groups/survivorsucks/viewtopic.php?f=74&t=132181&p=12637574&hilit=can%27t+wait+for+them+to+see#p12637574.

78 Kevin Michael DeLuca, *Image Politics: The New Rheotric of Environmental Activism* (New York, NY: The Guilford Press, 1999), 21–2.

79 Ibid., 305.

80 Judith Halberstam, *The Art of Queer Failure* (Durham, NC: Duke University Press, 2011), 17.

81 Ragan Fox, "'Phags for Phelps': Exploring the Queer Potential of the Westboro Baptist Church," *Liminalities: A Journal of Performance Studies* 11, no. 1 (2015): 4.

5
LIFE AFTER *BIG BROTHER*

In a blistering and hilarious essay about reality TV's relationship with celebrity, Jeffrey Sconce advocates the "almost unlimited potential and positive social utility" of the genre. He argues that reality competition series like *American Idol* theatricalize the "burnout trajectory of celebrity" into a condensed season of fleeting notoriety.[1] Reality TV programs market a rhetoric of aspiration that Pramaggiore and Negra contend forges "common ground with an audience that longs to believe in the class-mobility narrative that neoliberalism has made practically obsolete."[2] Reality TV hopefuls may find its neoliberal trap especially seductive given the rare success stories of a few genre participants, like *The Real Housewives of New York*'s Bethenny Frankel and *American Idol*'s Kelly Clarkson. Reflecting on Frankel's *Housewives*-launched Skinnygirl brand empire, Suzanne Leonard and Diane Negra claim that, "Frankel's success illustrates that economies of self can be leveraged" and result in substantial financial gain.[3]

Compared to Bravo, which is Frankel's home network, CBS fosters a much different relationship with its reality TV talent. The network's odd antagonism toward its stable of onscreen personalities first became obvious to me when *Survivor* stopped airing opening credits that feature the names of the season's participants. Episodes once began with a 55-second slow-motion montage of contestants battling through the elements and in the midst of exotically back-dropped competitions. Each survivor's name flashed onscreen as their image emerged. Removing the names and images of contestants in the opening credits underscores CBS's philosophy regarding reality TV participants: We are transitory and our personalities and potential should never eclipse the passing and limited opportunity the network provides us.

People featured on network reality programs deal with the emotional toll of public scrutiny without the fantastic benefits of celebrity. Reflecting on reality

126 Life After *Big Brother*

TV's revised "calculus of celebrity," Biressi and Nunn suggest that, "'Ordinary' stars of reality shows acquire massive media visibility but possess very little in the way of institutional power or control."[4] Despite *Survivor's* pre-tax $1 million and *Big Brother's* $500,000 grand prizes, many contestants lose income when they agree to partake in televised competition. After winning $20,000 for performing two weeks of sabotage in the house, I earned a pre-tax total of $28,535 for my stint on *Big Brother*. Had it not been for my run as saboteur, CBS would have cut me a check for a whopping $8,535, which is what most of the other *Big Brother 12* jury members made for their three months of day-and-night labor. Factor in three months of missed pay and many *Big Brother 12* houseguests operated "in the red," or at a financial loss.

Big Brother's economics have proven significantly more perilous for contestants who found themselves unemployed after the show's completion. Days before the *Big Brother 15* finale, *The Atlantic* featured a story titled, "All Three *Big Brother* Finalists Have Been Fired from their Jobs for Being Racist." The article's author takes delight in the news, writing, "No matter who takes the prize, they're all losers."[5] Some firings are more understandable than others. The United Autism Foundation justifiably sacked Season 9 winner Adam Jasinski after he referred to autistic children as "retards." *Big Brother 12's* Rachel confessed to me that Las Vegas's Aria Resort and Casino let her go from her job as a VIP cocktail waitress because they feared she would bring unwanted attention to their clientele. In one of Season 13's more heartbreaking moments, Rachel revealed on the 24-hour live feed that she could not find work for nearly a year because nobody wanted to hire the villain from *Big Brother 12*. Rachel's shortcomings hardly warranted the employment nightmare she faced upon returning to the "real" world.

The economic potential of participants on shows like *Big Brother* "extends only as far as the specific 'reality' they have been recruited to enact."[6] There's a knee-jerk tendency among scholars and media critics—myself included—to assume reality television is not reality. But participating on a reality show results in undeniable, ongoing consequences that affect the material lives of its players. For every Bethenny Frankel success story, there are thousands of onscreen performers who walked away with less than that with which they entered their respective program.

Moreover, CBS is doggedly opposed to former *Big Brother* houseguests participating on other networks' television programs. My contract prevented me from joining the cast of a non-CBS affiliated show—reality or otherwise—for three years. Non-compete clauses are now illegal in the state of California and make little sense in an industry partially defined by how elusive it is to find work. The clause's sharp teeth dared to bite me only months after *Big Brother 12's* finale when I made it to the latter rounds of casting for Logo's never-launched *The A-List: Los Angeles*, a reality show that would follow the lives of up-and-coming gay professionals in West Hollywood. I furiously searched through a dizzying web of mass media ownership to see how CBS and Logo might be connected. Eureka! Viacom owns both networks. Hammering out a solution to CBS's contractual obligations proved to be an exercise in futility. Logo never ordered a run of *The A-List: Los Angeles* and I doubt I would have ultimately been cast. I sometimes wonder, though, how CBS would have reacted had Logo asked me to participate. Similar thoughts and questions emerge throughout the concluding chapter of this book. What is life like after *Big Brother*? How does one navigate the liminal space between anonymity and reality TV "fame"? What role do fans play in the lives of former houseguests? How does CBS continue to exert control over the post-show lives of houseguests? What are some of the neoliberal workings that ensnare reality TV participants?

I specifically reflect on what Vicki Mayer calls "the new television economy," or a "political and economic formation that uses Hollywood's cultural value to get people to do work without expectation of a material benefit or compensation for their labor."[7] I also consider the quotidian nature of reality TV celebrity and the racial and sexual politics that determine the kind of players asked to return to future seasons of *Big Brother*.

Minute 16

The year following my stint on *Big Brother*, strangers often asked for pictures and posed questions about my involvement on the program. I imagined a bright aura, or luster, around me—especially when I traveled out of Los Angeles. "Are you friends with Rachel or do you two still hate one another," most people asked. Other fans parroted statements I made in the house. "Count your friends in the house. Done already?" one lady joked, imitating what I said to Rachel when she returned to the house for 24 hours. I *was* the guy on a television show. I emphasize "was" because *Big Brother* is one of the only TV programs where the cast does not re-enter the world and interact with the public until after the season wraps. Contestants on *Survivor* and *The Amazing Race* finish taping months before their season premieres on CBS. *Big Brother* houseguests are not afforded the same opportunity. After the finale, CBS representatives unceremoniously shove houseguests in a taxi and release us back to the wild. We have no idea if production edited us to look like heroes or scoundrels. I will never forget Rachel's earnest shock when she realized she was Season 12's villain.

Reality TV's momentary taste of fame is intoxicating—especially for the attention-seeking men and women who participate. For the better part of a year, my life revolved around *Big Brother*. I was a guest on podcasts dedicated to the show, attended reality TV "star"-studded fundraisers, and talked endlessly about my experiences as a houseguest. Perhaps no better anecdote encapsulates the pseudo-celebrity of reality television than my experience at 2010's Hollywood Style Awards. The head of a vodka company gave Kristen, one of my closest friends from *Big Brother*, an invite and plus-one to the event. We had nothing better to do and thought attending would be an adventure. We would get to see actual celebrities doing what they do best—giving awards to one another. Upon

128 Life After *Big Brother*

our arrival, Mr. Vodka, who was partially sponsoring the event, informed us that we would not be able to sit in the auditorium during the awards show. "You'll have to sit in the lobby, but there are big-screen TVs out here," he explained. Mr. Vodka approached us 15 minutes later and demanded that we walk the red carpet with him. Kristen and I quickly figured out that we were his Z-list ticket to getting snapped by paparazzi.

This was my first time walking in front of a step-and-repeat, or publicity backdrop used in event photography. A red carpet's mechanics are dizzying. A Studio-54-like group of event producers tasked with determining which attendees are red-carpet worthy approve each person who walks down the crimson mat. If you make the cut, you wait in a long line as each luminary takes his or her turn walking past a velvet rope and standing in front of the step-and-repeat as hundreds of camera flashbulbs flicker. The TV or movie personality then walks a few steps, stops, stands in place, forces a smile or sexy look, and gets blinded once again by paparazzi. Shampoo, rinse, repeat.

I felt completely out of place the moment we stepped into line behind the likes of pop sensation Selena Gomez, movie actor Kate Bosworth, and Academy Award nominee Emily Blunt. Each passing moment catapulted me further back to anonymity and obscurity. I was only able to catch my breath when Mr. Vodka introduced us to the TV personality standing directly behind us. "Hi, I'm Ragan," I said as I offered the woman my hand for a shake. Neither Kristen nor I recognized her but Mr. Vodka assured us that she was "somebody too." "My name is Poprah," she declared. "Poprah?" I asked. "Yes, like poor Oprah. I was on the VH1 show *I Want to Work for Diddy*," Poprah explained. Kristen and I looked at one another, cracked half-smiles, and nodded. Poprah informed us that she is no stranger to the red carpet. "You get used to it," she consoled. An event producer broke up our conversation to inform us that we were next on the carpet.

Kristen, Mr. Vodka, and I took our first glorious step in front of the paparazzi's firing line. The photographers immediately transitioned from screaming Kate Bosworth's name and furiously capturing her image to near-radio silence. The twinkling lights of their cameras faded into a painful darkness, a lightless midnight that reminded me that I was no Kate Bosworth. To make matters worse, the ebb-and-flow of a step-and-repeat demand compliance, so we had to take two steps and relive the horror every two minutes.

One of the perils of being a houseguest is the realization that by the time the season concludes and CBS sends you home, you are already a has-been before you got to be an *is*. Because the show unfolds in near-real time, *Big Brother* contestants only get to taste their proverbial 15 minutes of fame at the start of minute 16. My faux-fame sheen began to tarnish six months after Season 12's finale and all but disappeared by fall 2011. I felt like a punctured balloon slowly spitting out air, or cultural currency.

Before each contestant enters the house, casting director Robyn Kass visits our hotel rooms and cautions us about life after the game. She encourages us to go back to our lives and appreciate the *Big Brother* experience for what it is, namely a once-in-a-lifetime opportunity to attend adult summer camp and have our adventures broadcast to the world. Robyn's advice hints at two types of former houseguests. One group is largely consumed and defined by *Big Brother*. The houseguest's Twitter feed is usually a strong indicator of their investment. Years after their stint on the show, they regularly post pictures of themselves in the house and post near-daily messages about the show. People in the second group go back to the business of living their lives. They return to their day jobs and likely no longer watch *Big Brother*.

Most new friends learn I was on the show several months after we meet. I rarely self-disclose that I am a reality TV has-been. *Big Brother* made me value my privacy and anonymity. Being the center of attention is no longer a concern. I ended production of my podcast a few years after Season 12 and have not engaged in live performance in several years. I even stopped watching *Big Brother* after Season 15. For me, the fifteenth installment's assortment of racist and homophobic houseguests killed the show's lighthearted joy. I also got tired of fans and former houseguests baiting me into online battles.

Season 8 winner Dick Donato waged digital war with me at the start of Season 14. A couple of weeks before the premiere, CBS announced that four houseguests would return to the show. Each returnee would coach a small team of new competitors. CBS's Web team created a poll on CBS.com, where they asked fans to vote on which four houseguests they thought would be invited back. I was one of 16 past competitors included as potential returnees. CBS never informed me that I would be part of the poll, which had no influence on who would return. Its only function was to spark viewer curiosity and publicize the upcoming season. The four returning houseguests were already in sequester by the time CBS published the survey. Annoyed by my unwilling inclusion, I never encouraged anyone to vote for me. Despite my inaction, the poll indicated viewers believed I would be among the four returning players. The results surprised me much the same way I was shocked to learn viewers voted for me to be Season 12's saboteur. Executive producer Rich Meehan pointed out that I was the first gay houseguest to win America's vote. Moreover, *Big Brother* has a terrible track record when it comes to inviting sexual minorities back to play an additional CBS-aired season. Producers have brought players back to play an additional regular Season 30 times but they have only invited a gay contestant to return and play again one time. The list of returnees indicates that sexual orientation consciously or subconsciously plays a hand in who gets a second or even third chance to play *Big Brother*. In terms of the poll results, a gay man outperforming a heterosexual former winner was certain to spark ire.

130   Life After *Big Brother*

My popularity in the poll angered Evel Dick, who repeatedly encouraged fans to vote for him in the CBS promotion and believed I should not be ranked higher than Season 2 champ Will Kirby. I responded to Dick's attack by noting his physical likeness to a zombie and pointing out how sad it is to care about the results of a poll that had no impact on which players would return. Four days later, I received Google notifications that I was in a Twitter war with Dick. One of the links Google provided featured participants in a *Big Brother* forum who claimed our alleged battle started after I Tweeted that I was a better player than Will Kirby. Dick was simply putting me in my place. I, of course, never argued that I was more deserving than Will. When this off-season exchange is placed next to Dick's mistreatment of other gay *Big Brother* contestants like Season 8's Dustin (who he repeatedly taunted with the name "princess"), Season 15's Andy (who is the only gay man to win *Big Brother* and whose victory Dick constantly characterizes as "the worst win ever"), and Season 16's Frankie (who is the repeated object of Dick's death fantasies), the implication is that a White, heterosexual, and homophobic man is the corrective required to silence gay men who respond to his bullying. Another link in a Google notification revealed that Dick produced a longwinded, unhinged video where he threatened me and encouraged his followers to find my phone number and address.

Dick tends to instigate battles with former houseguests at the start of each new *Big Brother* season. Dick's interpersonal drama with other houseguests drives people to his Web site and subscription-based Internet program *Dick at Night*, a video podcast in which he rants about current happenings in the *Big Brother* house. Still, Dick's call to violence paralyzed me. My home address is easy to discover and *Big Brother* devotees have a history of harassing ex-houseguests. Moreover, the conflict seemed utterly juvenile. Dick and his fans baited me into an argument about a poll on CBS.com. I took a few retaliatory shots at him and suddenly I am in an online war. To modify Michael Corleone in *The Godfather III*, "Just when I thought I was out of *Big Brother*, they pull me back in." My feud with Dick proved to be a pivotal moment. For me, the sparring crossed a line when he encouraged fans to locate my home address. I worried that somebody might show up at my door with a weapon, or track me down as I walked my dog. Staying on social media seemed like a terrible idea, so I signed off Twitter for a month, avoided *Big Brother* fan forums, and decided to skip Season 14, even though Britney, one of my closest friends from Season 12, returned as one of the coaches.

Fear consumed me. Each night, I took at least six trips to my front door to make sure it was locked. My brain understood the door was bolted but my emotions beckoned, "What if the door is unlocked? What if tonight is the night a crazed fan breaks in and kills you?" The monologue forced me out of bed and back to the door. Irrational fear creeped into other aspects of my life. I feared somebody might poison my food if I left it unattended. Acting in accordance with fear only enhanced my anxiety. The more I double-checked my front door and discarded food, the more nervous I became. By the end of August 2012,

Life After *Big Brother* **131**

I lived in a near-perpetual state of panic. The situation grew so dire that I made an emergency appointment with a psychiatrist who diagnosed me with Obsessive-Compulsive Disorder. In retrospect, I had spent most of my adult life battling moderate OCD. Anxiety only reached the level of "disorder" that summer, when irrational, sustained angst interfered with my everyday life.

I should have started seeing a therapist the day CBS shoved me in a cab and sent me back to West Hollywood. My brain was not operating properly. I was used to seeing fewer than 12 people a day, and my synapses were not prepared to be wired back into a fast-paced, digital world where endless news updates and media stories ping phones every hour. Even eating dinner at a restaurant felt like a Herculean task. All the loud conversations and people overwhelmed me. Other houseguests from my season reported similar mental impairments, like the sudden onset of agoraphobia, or fear of crowds, and forgetfulness. I now recognize that our malfunctioning brains were symptomatic of ongoing solitary confinement, food restrictions, and other forms of unusual punishment disguised as entertainment. Mechanisms designed to make *Big Brother*'s players more reactive, or dramatic, proved significant enough to exacerbate my underlying anxiety problems. Likewise, Dick's threats acted as the proverbial straw that broke my back, or brain. Where was Dr. Jakobs when I needed her?

The Reality TV-Industrial Complex

Big Brother is one-third of CBS's reality television-industrial complex. I characterize *Big Brother*, *Survivor*, and *The Amazing Race* as an "industrial complex" to highlight how CBS executives exploit reality TV's onscreen talent. Reality TV participants are an inexpensive labor force—a disorganized group of men and women who are not protected by a union and unfamiliar with the ramifications of their involvement. Reality TV-industrial complex pays homage to military-industrial complex, a term that describes a bilateral relationship between a nation's military and the for-profit companies that arm it. Scholars have used the industrial complex metaphor to characterize phenomena ranging from medical professionals working with drug companies to push specific pharmaceuticals (i.e., the medical-industrial complex) to the state turning imprisonment into a for-profit endeavor (i.e., the prison-industrial complex). Industrial complex carries an exploitative connotation intended to highlight how powerful people use technology to financially take advantage of groups with less power. Less powerful groups in this context include both reality TV's onscreen talent and television actors, costumers, and writers, among others, who have been pressured to work more for less to compete with reality TV's slim production costs.

The 2007–8 Writers Guild of America strike illustrates how network executives have used reality television to financially manipulate unionized talent. The Writers Guild labor union represents U.S.-based film, TV, and radio writers. Guild members went on strike for 100 days from November 2007 until February 2008

132 Life After *Big Brother*

to secure fair compensation for their work when it reaches home video markets, such as DVD and digital media. The strike resulted in a blackout of new scripted television and thousands of layoffs. CBS, NBC, ABC, and FOX relied on unscripted programs to fill the void of sitcoms and dramas. That winter and spring, CBS aired its only regular-season broadcast of *Big Brother*. The networks' collective message was clear: scripted genres are replaceable. The Writers Guild moved to expand its membership to include reality program story producers. So-called unscripted shows require teams of people to collect and edit raw footage into a logical narrative complete with protagonists, antagonists, and story arcs. The organization eventually dropped its request to include reality TV story producers among its rank-and-file.

The strike demonstrates how reality TV functions as a neoliberal industrial complex in two key ways. First, network executives have repeatedly pit scripted programming against reality shows. Their suggestion is that everyday people can replace skilled actors and writers. The threat of substitution is then used as a bargaining chip to fill the coffers of men like Les Moonves by ensuring that actors, writers, and TV show staff earn less. Second, members of the Writers Guild rightfully battled for reasonable payment of their work. But their struggle only underscores how beholden reality TV writers and performers are to media executives. Reality TV participants are not unionized. The entire genre, in fact, is premised on Andy Warhol's 15-minutes-of-fame prophecy. The fleeting popularity of individual reality show participants makes it virtually impossible to organize or demand adequate pay. While writers and actors fight for greater DVD royalties, *Big Brother* houseguests are not even provided with a free copy of the season in which they participated. I had to purchase my season on iTunes to view it.

Nick Couldry notes that *Big Brother* exemplifies neoliberal subjugation and constitutes a theater of cruelty. There is no better way to characterize a system that "requires of its participants' continuous loyalty, submission to surveillance and external direction even within the deepest recesses of private life, yet demands of those same individuals an acceptance of the fragility and impermanence of the opportunity it provides."[8] Expectations of loyalty and submission to CBS continue long after houseguests return to their regular lives. *Big Brother* producers dangle the chance of future participation to keep past houseguests silent about industry secrets. Robyn Kass, for instance, learned Rachel and Brendon divulged to Season 12's Matt they were entering sequester for Season 13. CBS goes to great lengths to conceal the identities of each cast member until late June, when anchors for CBS's *The Early Show* reveal the competitors' names. Robyn immediately informed Matt and other past houseguests that anyone who revealed names of past competitors returning for Season 13 would not get to return for an All-Stars season of the program. Production's hypothetical blacklist is powerful enough to silence even *Big Brother*'s most loose-lipped players. The warning's ability to mute a large group of garrulous men and women is absurd given that the series has only conducted one All-Stars season in its 19-year run. Instead, *Big*

Life After *Big Brother*   **133**

Brother has aired multiple hybrid seasons where a group of returning players is mixed in with a larger collection of new competitors.

Production's threat of a blacklist never intimidated me. They have only allowed one gay houseguest to return to a regular season. This sad statistic has never been lost on me. CBS enthusiastically invites back players who fell in love on the show. The catch, of course, is that heterosexual people are the only contestants permitted to have an intimate relationship in the house because, overwhelmingly, seasons only include a single lesbian and/or gay man. Popular characters who can performatively enact their heterosexuality are routinely asked to participate on other CBS reality shows. *Big Brother* power couples are a regular fixture on *The Amazing Race*, which has featured Season 11 and 13's Jeff and Jordan, Season 12 and 13's Rachel and Brendon, and Season 19's Jessica and Cody. Season 12 winner Hayden became the first *Big Brother* houseguest to compete on a season of *Survivor* after CBS executives discovered he was dating a former *Survivor* castaway named Kat. Hayden and Kat competed as lovers on *Survivor's* "Blood vs. Water" season.

Entire challenges have been dedicated to *Big Brother's* celebration of heterosexuality. Producers created a Season 12 veto competition called "Lovers Lane" that celebrated Jeff and Jordan finding love in the *Big Brother* house the previous summer. Jeff and Jordan returned to the backyard for one day to host the bowling-themed game. Red and pink flowers and cut-out hearts adorned the backyard. Game producers even painted the bowling pins pastel pink and blue—colors that symbolize the announcement of baby girls and boys. Season 15's second veto competition centered around the pregnancy of Season 12 and 14's Britney. In the episode, contestants gather around a television in the living room, where a pre-recorded tape of Britney is played. "I have some big news," she teases. "I'm having a baby." The camera zooms out to reveal Britney's full stomach and a crib. The competitors laugh, clap, and cheer at Britney's successful execution of heteronormativity. Britney continues, "I need everyone to get to the backyard and help me get my nursery together." The backyard resembles a huge nursery, complete with oversized toys, crayons, stuffed animals, blocks, and cribs. Players are assigned a crib, where they must hang an assortment of stuffed animals on a baby's mobile. The first person to perfectly balance ten toys on the apparatus wins the game. Production has tasked the houseguests with building a metaphorical shrine to Britney's pregnancy. I struggle to imagine *Big Brother* inviting me back to the show to discuss my use of a surrogate or adoption of a child, nor can I visualize CBS constructing a competitive apparatus to commemorate my plutonic friendship with Season 12's Matt—despite their repeated suggestion that there might be something more to our relationship. *Big Brother* competitions theatricalize and reinforce the traditional gender binary and heteronormative sexuality. Reflecting on the gendered and sexed aspects of games and sports, Shogan and Davidson argue that, "These performances produce particular notions of sexed bodies—permeable, penetrable females and impermeable, penetrating males—and notions of what counts as sexual practice linked to these notions of sexed bodies.

134 Life After *Big Brother*

One is either heterosexually male or female."[9] *Big Brother*'s carnival of heteronormative performativity is what Butler might describe as a "regulated process of repetition,"[10] where each season's dominant narrative focuses on a heterosexual showmance, only gender-conforming houseguests are invited to participate in other CBS reality shows and multiple seasons of *Big Brother*, and competitions function as monuments to heteronormativity. Conversely, LGBTQ participants are not asked to return, a gesture that symbolizes homosexuality's failure to repeat or reproduce.

Repetition is one of performativity's key components. It matters that, time and again, *Big Brother* invites heterosexual contestants to return to the game. Intended or not, the suggestion is that only straight houseguests are worth seeing beyond their initial season. The more a competitor uses *Big Brother*'s stage to performatively and explicitly enact his or her heterosexuality, the more likely he or she is to return for additional seasons and be cast on other CBS reality shows. Game designers building challenges around past players' heteronormative milestones, like marriage and pregnancy, only bolster the program's commitment to neoliberalism. Reproduction—in all its connotations—is a battery that powers CBS's neoliberal machine. *Big Brother* contestants are rewarded for their ability to reproduce hegemonic cultural structures. The more literal the reproduction (e.g., meeting on the show, getting married, and producing a child), the more valuable the contestant. Rachel and Brendon and Jeff and Jordan met on the *Big Brother* set, married after their respective seasons, and had children. It is no mistake that CBS has offered the most financial opportunities and exposure to the four houseguests who enacted heterosexuality's two primary milestones (i.e., marriage and reproduction). Jeff and Jordan have both appeared on the CBS soap opera *The Bold and the Beautiful* and competed on a season of *The Amazing Race* and two seasons of *Big Brother*. Rachel and Brendon have also appeared on *The Bold and the Beautiful*, along with both competing on two seasons of *Big Brother* and two seasons of *The Amazing Race*. Moreover, Rachel and Jordan have both won a season of *Big Brother*.

Sexual minorities on the show offer a bleak point of comparison. As discussed in Chapter 3, *Big Brother*'s story producers often perpetuate the myth that LGBTQ contestants are disconnected from family through their symbolic annihilation of queer competitors' loved ones. LGBTQ houseguests rarely receive a friends-and-family package when they make it to the latter stages of the game. Even the sole gay competitor to win the grand prize did not receive a segment featuring his relatives and friends. Queer houseguests are included in nearly every season but their limited involvement in future seasons reproduces heteronormativity's logic and the flawed perception that homosexuality is fleeting and in need of containment. To modify Judith Halberstam, the neoliberal and capitalist underpinnings of the program mark the

> homosexual as somehow failed, as the subject who fails to embody the connections between production and reproduction. Capitalist logic casts

the homosexual as inauthentic and unreal, as incapable of proper love and unable to make the appropriate connections between sociality, relationality, family, sex, desire, and consumption.[11]

Reflecting on Reflections

Inside Reality TV represents how I have chosen to bid adieu to nearly a decade of my life largely been defined by my involvement in *Big Brother*. Writing about my experiences has given me insight I need to let go of the absurd notion that *Big Brother* producers control my life story, to abandon hurt feelings that emerged after reading homophobic viewer comments, to relinquish rage that rushed over my body as I witnessed Season 15's spectacle of racism, and to concede that I will never be invited back to another season. I also acknowledge the wealth of opportunity my participation on *Big Brother* offered. The research essay upon which this book is premised is the all-time most downloaded article in my field (Communication Studies). I am under no illusion that the article's 25,904 hits can be attributed to my profound argumentation skills or writing style. The text's popularity is largely a result of the economics of being on and writing about a reality show that has millions of viewers. My built-in audience also partially explains why academic book publishers are interested in my post-show reflections. Hearn argues that when "viewers become [reality TV] participants they are not only labourers for the television industry, but have also become image-entrepreneurs, representing the ultimate socialization of labour."[12]

John Corner ends his canonical essay "Performing the Real" by cautioning readers against simplifying the relationship between *Big Brother*'s "representational system and its commodity functions."[13] My autoethnographic account of auditioning for, competing on, watching, and making sense of life after *Big Brother* provides a narrative blueprint that maps the precise ways the program's representational mechanisms transform television viewers into objects of media consumption and forms of inexpensive labor. The program's manufactured absences expose the iterative limits of reality TV's machine of representation, or the moments its performative instruments sputter and break down. *Big Brother*'s voids of representation call attention to connections Corner draws between representation and commodity. Each absence is a spark, or rupture, that reveals the contingencies upon which sexual minorities and people of color may participate on a program like *Big Brother*. Spark → I can be gay on the show as long as the physical mechanics of my sexuality are never staged. Spark → Dramatic depictions of in-house racism will only be constructed if viewers threaten to boycott; and when those narratives finally emerge, racism is conveniently located in one or two contestants as narrated by a third racist houseguest whose sustained prejudice is strategically erased by producers.

136 Life After *Big Brother*

I started this book promising to detail how *Big Brother's* production team, fans, and participants performatively render LGBTQ houseguests and contestants of color. Our performances of marginality are contingent upon an imposed and simultaneous perception that we are mere stereotypes—boiled-down replicas of all queer people and people of color—*and*, paradoxically, failures to "represent our communities." Because men and women from historically marginalized groups are placed in the *Big Brother* house with casts that are primarily White and heterosexual, the very people tasked with narrating gay tears and Black rage tell their tales from a privileged location, where representations of whiteness and heterosexuality are rarely called into question.

This is not to say racist and homophobic ruptures in reality TV go wholly unnoticed and unchallenged. *Big Brother* is in part remarkable because it is one of the rare programs that allows its audience to view hundreds of hours of unaired footage every season. *Big Brother's* live feed provides audiences a partial glance into what Goffman might describe as reality TV's backstage performances. Backstage voyeurism is the instrument that enables *Big Brother's* audience to intervene when its broadcast narrative becomes problematic. When producers had Season 15's Amanda narrate Aaryn's and GinaMarie's racism, one live-feed viewer created a six-minute montage of Amanda's numerous racist and homophobic moments. The video titled "Amanda Zuckerman: Social Justice Warrior" has been viewed nearly 350,000 times on YouTube and includes a description that reads:

> CBS has aired some of Aaryn's racism, but in the process made Amanda out to be some sort of hero/social justice warrior, calling out all the racism in the house. Clearly, this is not the case. Amanda is one of the worst and most unrepentant offenders in the house. This video only shows a small fraction of her horrible comments.[14]

Questions of audience interactivity, like the YouTube video calling out Amanda's racism, drive *Inside Reality TV*.

Su Holmes believes reality TV's audience interactivity provides a "promise of 'power' [that] clearly has political significance."[15] Audience-text intertextuality is especially important to explore in the context of reality TV because the mode of entertainment is premised upon the genre's audience acting as eventual onscreen participants. *Inside Reality TV's* investment in performative spectatorship enabled me to recognize how *Big Brother's* illusions of democracy (e.g., demographics, "ordinary" players, and vote-based eliminations) are only realized by the show's audience-text dynamism, or the tendency for viewers to rally against the program's egalitarian fiction.

Fan-produced commentary may even have more of an impact on reality TV production than Media Studies criticism. Through its celebration of secondary texts, performative spectatorship acknowledges the ways in which audience members construct what Halberstam describes as low theory. Low theory reaches an audience that is often unpersuaded by high theory, or the sort of academic writing that requires advanced degrees to understand. During Season 13 of *Big Brother*, I wrote several blog entries that critiqued viewers comparing Kalia to an ape. *Survivor* Sucks members mocked my critique of racism in their forums. They complained that my arguments were longwinded. I used too many big words. They were put off by my academese, or dry, complicated language. In retrospect, I understand their frustration. Footnotes and parenthetical citations repel men and women who immediately dismiss posts longer than a paragraph with "TLDR," or "too long, didn't read."

As outlined in Chapter 4, the same community engaged in anti-racist critique two years later through the production of Photoshopped images comparing racist *Big Brother* houseguests to Klan members and anti-integrationists from the 1950s. Halberstam recognizes that low theory is not just a matter of accessibility, but "we might also think about it as a kind of theoretical model that flies below the radar, that is assembled from eccentric texts and examples and that refuses to confirm the hierarchies of knowing that maintain the *high* in high society."[16] People active in the *Survivor* Sucks forum do more than author scathing attacks of houseguests; they *theorize* about *Big Brother*. Their posts function as a shadow text that lingers just under the program's main body.

My relationship with *Big Brother*'s audience has not been uniform. Some viewers love me, others despise me (and probably even more have forgotten I was a contestant). Regardless of where I fall on their love–hate scale, I hope that *Inside Reality TV* will help viewers humanize *Big Brother* contestants and reveal the rhetorical traps that entangle houseguests in modes of representation they often actively resist. I am ready to close the book (so to speak) on *Big Brother*.

Cut to Big Brother's *memory wall, where Ragan's color portrait fades to black and white.*

Notes

1 Jeffrey Sconce, "See You in Hell, Johnny Bravo!" *Reality TV: Remaking Television Culture*, ed. Susan Murray and Laurie Ouellette (New York, NY: New York University Press, 2004), 256.

2 Maria Pramaggiore and Diane Negra, "Keeping Up with the Aspirations: Commercial Family and the Kardashian Brand," *Reality Gendervision: Sexuality and Gender on Transatlantic Reality Television* (Durham, NC: Duke University Press, 2014), 82.

3 Suzanne Leonard and Diane Negra, "Bethenny Frankel, Self-Branding, and the 'New Intimacy of Work," *Cupcakes, Pinterest, and Ladyporn: Feminized Popular Culture in the Early Twenty-First Century* (Champaign, IL: University of Illinois, 2015), 196.

4 Anita Biressi and Heather Nunn, *Reality TV: Realism and Revelation* (New York, NY: Wallflower Press, 2005), 148.

5 Brian Moylan, "All Three Big Brother Finalists Have Been Fire from Their Jobs for Being Racist," *The Atlantic*, last modified September 16, 2013, accessed March 29, 2018, www.theatlantic.com/entertainment/archive/2013/09/all-three-big-brother-final ists-have-been-fired-their-jobs-being-racist/311047/.

138 Life After *Big Brother*

6 Alison Hearn, "'John, a 20-Year-Old Boston Native with a Great Sense of Humor': ON the Spectacularization of the 'Self' and the Incorporation of Identity in the Age of Reality Television," 143.

7 Vicki Mayer, "Cast-aways: The Plights and Pleasures of Reality Casting and Production Studies," *A Companion to Reality Television* (Malden, MA: Wiley Blackwell, 2017), 64.

8 Nick Courdry, "Reality TV, or the Secret Theatre of Neoliberalism," *Education, Pedagogy and Cultural Studies* 30, no. 1 (2008): 3.

9 Debra Shogan and Judy Davidson, "Parody of the Gay Games: Gender Performativity in Sport," *Journal of the Canadian Lesbian and Gay Studies Association* 1 (1999): 90.

10 Judith Butler, *Gender Trouble: Feminism and the Subversion of Identity* (New York, NY: Routledge, 1990), 145.

11 Judith Halberstam, *The Queer Art of Failure* (Durham, NC: Duke University Press, 2011).

12 Alison Hearn, "'John, a 20-Year-Old Boston Native with a Great Sense of Humor': ON the Spectacularization of the 'Self' and the Incorporation of Identity in the Age of Reality Television," *International Journal of Media and Cultural Politics* 2, no. 2 (2006): 136.

13 John Corner, "Performing the Real: Documentary Diversions," 268.

14 "Amanda Zuckerman: Social Justice Warrior," *YouTube*, last modified July 31, 2013, accessed March 30, 2018, www.youtube.com/watch?v=LcmnVw-RQM0.

15 Su Holmes, "'But This Time You Choose!' Approaching the 'Interactive Audience' in Reality TV," *International Journal of Cultural Studies* 7, no. 2 (2004): 214.

16 Judith Halberstam, *The Queer Art of Failure*, 16.

INDEX

The Amazing Race 15, 52, 118, 127
arguments 77, 79
authenticity 2, 9, 13–14, 31, 43
autoethnography 3, 32, 55, 135

The Bachelor 7, 16, 97, 113
bullying 8, 57, 79

casting: application 29; archetypes 43–4;
  casting call audition 7, 27–9; finals 31,
  33–42, 44; interviews 29–30, 40–2,
  46, 49; protocol 43, 45, 47; semi-finals
  29–30; tests 38–9
celebrity *see* fame
Chen, Julie 56, 64, 119–20
competition 5–7, 15, 134; eviction 6–7,
  84, 100, 119–20; have-nots 6, 56–8, 80;
  Head of Household 5, 56–7, 72, 79;
  nominations 5–6, 58–9; Power of Veto
  6, 59, 80–1
contract 12, 25, 126

diary room 58–60, 79–80, 82–3
Duck Dynasty 9, 44

economics 126–7, 131–2, 135
employment: firing 1–3
everyday life performance 4, 24–5, 33, 52

fame 127–8, 132
fan commentary 135–6; textual
  commentary 55, 61–2, 70, 72, 100,

103–4; visual commentary 62–8, 72–8,
  100–3, 104–6, 109–11, 117
firing 126

heteronormativity 8, 15–16, 55, 56,
  133–4
homophobia 81–3, 113, 115, 130, 135–6
homosexuality *see* LGBTQ

labor 93
LGBTQ: anti-gay epithets 61, 70–1;
  crying gay man trope 56–9, 61; disease
  trope 61, 70–1; familial ties 12, 54,
  57, 71, 134–5; Femme bashing 70–4;
  flaming homosexual trope 58, 66;
  gay-by-association trope 62, 64; gay
  erasure (*see* produced absence); gay
  pretender trope 55; gay sidekick
  trope 33, 54; HIV narratives 12, 14;
  hyper-sexual trope 62, 66, 70–2, 75–8;
  intimacy 15–16, 54; lesbianism 8; mental
  illness trope 11, 64, 72; overdramatic
  stereotype 77; people of color 14, 16–17;
  social acceptance 11; tokenization 84–5;
  transgender 44; transphobia 65–6; villain
  trope 12, 55, 59–66

masculinity 41, 58–9, 64, 72

narration 115
narrative 43, 53, 55
narratization 52–5, 62, 64, 66, 85, 108

140 Index

neoliberalism 10, 20–2, 93, 125, 127, 132, 134
news media 13

panopticon 36–8, 47
people of color: allusions 100–1, 116–17; angry black woman stereotype 95–7; Asian Americans 113; bad mother stereotype 95–7; criminality 17–18; exoticization 103–8; Latinas 104–5, 108–10; monkey trope 98–103; monstrosity trope 108–13; racial conflict 17, 113–16; racial juxtaposition 17, 100, 107–8, 111; stereotypes of Black women 19, 104, 106; stereotypes of Italians 43–4; tokenization 18–19; unclean trope 103–4
performative spectatorship 19–20, 97–8, 116–20
performativity 9–11, 14, 71, 97, 134; peri-performativity 25, 27, 39–40, 44
performing not-performing 2, 9, 31, 48
produced absence 8, 54–5, 113–14, 118

producer manipulation 36–8, 43–4, 47–8, 60, 79–80, 82
psychiatry 34, 39–40, 130–1

Queer Eye for the Straight Guy 16, 54

racism 113–15, 135–7; *see also* people of color
The Real Housewives 19, 33, 125
reality TV-industrial complex 131–5
The Real World 14, 17, 38
returning players 129, 132–3

secrecy 30, 33–4, 36, 47
sequester 34–7
Sex & the City 33, 67
sexuality 8, 10–11
showmance 56, 59, 62, 92, 133
staged reality 9–10
surveillance 31, 38
Survivor 4, 15, 17–19, 52–3, 67, 125, 127

Twitter 77, 129–30

whiteness 5, 7–8, 17, 28, 97, 100, 108, 110
Will & Grace 33, 54, 67, 68, 86, 88